The path of love
is without end
if you value your life
then stay away

If you give your life,
then learn,
a thousand are
given in return.

Attar (Persia 12th Century)

RAVEN

WORDS TO BREAK YOU OPEN

Language is our prayer to the great mystery of being.

Sometimes we have no choice but to write, it's like a tornado has built up inside us and if we don't let rip with the whirlwind of words that are spinning in our soul, it will surely kill us.

As you will see, this is a book about eloquence and longing, inspired by the beautiful tradition of poetry and eloquent speech that goes beyond cultural boundaries, religion or belief systems.

To remember is to literally come back together, for us great amnesiacs are always forgetting that we are nature, we are the universe, we are divine and yet earth bodies forever gazing at the same essence, our true nature, yet simply dressed in our infinite potentials and possibilities, imagining that we are separate.

If we allow ourselves to become lost in the words, to go beyond concepts, beyond beliefs, beyond the idea of the self of who we think we are, we are able to see that we are all holding the most beautiful gift, which is ever present in the centre of our being.

We all love stories, as children we are fascinated by our imagination, adventures and epic journeys.

Story and poetry is a great gift that can take us back the very essence of who we are. Yet if we become too analytical, we can read hundreds of books, but still we miss the point. So, by using language to go beyond the imaginary constraints, the cultural pomposity or conceptual limitations, we can open our heart, as well as our mind and become the very music of life as it lives inside us, and touches the ancient chambers of the heart and soul.

In these words we find a language that can express that deep longing we all share, so when we reach that point where our body dissolves back into the mystery from which we all arose, we are able to look back at this exquisite gift of life with gratitude and appreciation.

This book is my attempt to share some of this language that goes beyond the usual mountain of words we digest every day. Here are words that hopefully express the incredible gift of life.

Some cultures believe that through language we have the opportunity to offer something beautiful and mysterious back to this world as an offering. And through this treasure of words, the divine may just hear the longing and grief that weaves the very contours of our heart.

By creating beautiful offerings with our words, the beloved responds by showing us the very beauty that we are, and by trying to express the beauty of our being, maybe, just maybe, we wake up!

With this in mind, I hope you enjoy this offering and through its tangled web you may also jump up and have the confidence to find that expression of your deepest soul on its way home.

Raven

This body is a house for stars,
keep the doors wide open
and in fly the ravens.

The moon shimmers on the inside,
the sun beats on the way out.

Every breathe a galaxy,
every heartbeat a universe,
beyond even that.

I fell.

<u>Pan Demic -
From the Greek; Pan
(All) Demos (People)</u>

And finally, the great ancient god of nature, of the wild places, of the mossy brooks and golden hills, of the damp forests and hidden glades. The protector of beasts, of horned and hoofed, of wild lichen eyebrows and musk deer pungent aroma, swirls in through the ether, playing his deep evocative rhythm of enchantment on his bone flute, from beyond the veils, from the under and other worlds, he curls his misty-eyed brow towards humanity once again, reminding them of their tiny insignificant lives are mere dewdrops on the vast garden of existence. All their self-help seminars and self-important narcissistic endeavours are nothing but the froth of waves on the infinite sun rays of existence.

You can wash your hands, but you cannot wash away the wild, the mysterious, the ravaging wild ferocious tenacity of the wild world. You can try and blame it on 5g or secret agendas, you can create as many concepts as you like, but in the end, nature will roar with wild and ecstatic bloodthirsty longing to take us all home to where we began. The deep dark emptiness, where everything arises and begins, time without end. Where our rainbow cup of tea spirituality is meaningless, futile and pointless against the vast infinite darkness that swallows whole empires and civilisations, never mind petty personalities and ideas of self, which wither away in the face of primordial presence.

Pan, the original horned god, once again steps out of the shadows, with his name on the tongues of all beings, pandemic, pandemonium, panic, panacea, all bursting forth like wild flowers yearning to kiss the sky. In this realm, there is no good or bad, high or low, rich or poor, just the wild abandoned expression of life and death, forever dancing in the orgasmic Milky Way of existence, radiant in its potential.

Turned into the devil by the Christian cult, for nature and its holy reverence was to be outcasted for the reverence of god in man's image rather than the ancient pagan rituals of honouring gods and goddesses in the holy rivers and springs, forests and mountain tops.

Yet no childish concept of a saviour god or ancient black shrine will save us from the wild and it's inevitable and irresistible force. For we are nature in our deepest dreaming, before we civilised ourselves into square boxes and ready meals. We are life and death, we are the earth woven lovers of the wild, we are that radiant mysterious emptiness, we are Pan, we are all people.

Listen to the call of all beings, deep in the dark of night, at the cusp of dawn or dusk. You will hear your ancient voice forever singing you back home....

Hush.....

The Coming Storm

The coming storm
Gathers
On the horizon
Of the mind

People
Pull up their
Concepts
To fend off life

Rain
Ravens curl
On the inside
No one
Wants
To know
The truth
Any longer

A wave

Takes time

To swallow

Salt tears

Are tiny fragments

Of longing

Compared

To the coming

storm

The public

Believe

Anything

Now

Anyone

That posts

A prayer

Is locked

Up

Immediately

By the mighty

Lords of judgement

You are
Either
With us
Or without
Town criers
Yell
From the high
Broken citadels
Of democracy

And the
Remnants
Of liberty
Lie
The bones
Of whales
And sea horses

All now
Lost

In the
Memory
Of man
Who
Tore down
Every creature's
Soul
With
His lies
And prophecies

The last tree
Hangs
To the last bear

Whilst
All around
People
Argue
Whether
The sun
Is real
Or created

By them
The ones
Who control
Everything
So it's said

Nobody
Listens
Any longer
To the secrets of
The waves

The depth of rain
The song of wind
Or lapwing
The caress of eagle
The midnight howl of wolf
Of roaring thunder songs
The hum of bees
Or flight of bat

They are
Too
Busying
Debating
Fake facts

Radical Ferocious Beauty

We are never going to save the earth and all its intricate beauty by persuading people to change their disposable coffee cups, recycle their teabag, or buying less toys. Yes, they may go a small way to feeling better about doing our bit, but ultimately, it's totally missing the point.

The essential problem is not in the objects, they are just symbolic of the root problem of grasping. Human beings are it seems, hard wired to grasp what they can. Maybe it's thousands of years living in caves or on the savannah, barely surviving feeling that there's never quite enough, maybe it's just a genetic impulse to survive or maybe it's an unconscious feeling of never quite being good enough.

Ironically symbolised by the religions and beliefs that have conjured up the concept of original sin.

That we always somehow must get better, build better castles and grander kingdoms.

This grasping is across the board, whether it's the rampant consumerism of Christmas, surely a cracking irony in itself, the need for recognition in business or education, the conquering of countries and the horrendous genocide of colonialism that followed, the endless wars across the ages or the simple moment recently when the crowd of well-meaning folk in a workshop grasped at the materials to make an offering like it was the end of the world. Getting stuff will never be enough

.

Surely it's only by realising that right here now, this moment is enough, that this is it. Not the next moment, not the past, not by getting something else, I will somehow be better, but realising that you are living on the cutting edge of all that insatiable creativity of the universe, and the gift of this life is to give something back to the world as a unique uncompromising offering of all the things one has learnt from both the failures, grief and longing.

Maybe this offering can be what saves the world from the insatiable grasping and greed of humanity, that its actually about giving something back, no matter how small or pathetic it seems, no matter how scary it seems.

To see that in reality life is always interwoven and inter connected to everything else, nothing lives in isolation, everything depends on everything else. It seems we are coming to a place where we don't really have much choice, the old ways of thinking of separation, isolation, nationalism, rise their heads like serpents from a quagmire of ignorance, yet the violence of their outdated models of thinking have no place if we are to survive.

The extinction of species and the very survival of the planet is at stake, rather than the politics of small mindedness, there is something much deeper in our being that draws to the depths of our deepest creative wisdom to rise up and reveal itself in all its radical ferocious beauty.

Dawn

Empty dark whale lover
Her deep dark body
Stretching from nowhere to everywhere
Yet
If you listen deeply
Tiny stars
Already gather inside you
Inside every winter are the shimmers
of spring and summer
Autumn is already calling you
home again
The songs start slowly and invite you
If you listen deeper
You will hear
The forest inside you
Where every last creature stirs
Your dark uneven nature is laid bare
The Wild has never left you
Old friend

All these concrete walls
and Netflix evenings
Will never wipe out the song of your
Ancestors yearning
The dark caves and fire light
midnights
Praying
The wet forests and vast journeys
Mammoth boned and sabre-toothed
voyageurs
The mightiest oak has its roots
In your heart
The deepest ocean is that which pulls
you under
And brings you back again
Someone once told you,
That the dark forests are
For strangers
Yet if you listen carefully
You can hear
the purr of jaguar
The roaring of ten thousand

Starlings

Beckoning

You to pray

With your bone laden prayer matt

Made from the toil

Of your father

And tears of your mother

Whilst Lord coyote smokes,

drinks and gambles beside you

Laughing

You are the unsurpassable raven

Let her break you

Not the way you want

This isn't a cacophony of self help

With Self-proclaimed elders awaiting

Singing

Praises to the self

Here the idea of you

is a distant memory

Not a temple to be adorned

By Human centric

Obsessivity

The earth is laden
Stripped bare
With that kind of
Power point philosophy
The religion of narcissism
Nicely packaged
In neat white gowns
With slides and presentations
Of how you could be better
If only
You don't get mud on your shoes
Here the invitation
Is not to be anything
But the moisture of a thousand
rain filled midnights
Of the wild deer forever
following the morning star
Across mountain lakes and the earth

laden
dreams of Poseidon

Of twisted bark and
howling wolves yearning
Of all that's dying, and longing, crying
To live, unfettered, unadorned,
ravaged by beauty
Untouched by maidens
dressed in holy veils
Singing mantras
Given by gurus
Who sit on impassable high thrones
With their tiny pictures of saints
And sticks of nagchampa
Of self-imposed avatars
And their samosa shaped armies
Singing designated holy songs
To hollow chambers
Where nothing wild and erotic lives
Where sanitised shopping centres
Merge with consumerist deities
Symbols become the gods
Of youth and their knife blade tongues
Rapping their way

To bling laden promises
Whilst down in the highways
Of mediocrity
Old people hustle and listen
Around boxes
To the voices of saviours
Dressed in pin striped robes
Praying to the past
Of empire dreaming
As if
Cups of Ceylon will Save us
From the fire
All day long
The soothsayers
Speak
Fake
News
Up and down Albion
Gangsters peddle tunes
To the willing
Cheap melodies
Of a better time

As Anglo-Saxon heretics

Hear how immigrants

Will ruin this country

Let's long

For beef curries

And tea leaf

Prophecies

Two by two

As if Noah's ark

Is back in fashion

Yet all around

The deep wild

Is waiting

Silence never leaves us

We have been taught

In these colleges of concept

That

Thinking

Will save us

Somehow

Make us holy

That the unkempt

And mysterious

Is far too

Dangerous

To

Hear

Yet

Deep in the majesty of being

Are a thousand lovers

Gathering at your shore

Praying for your return

There are whales diving

Deep inside your tempestuous oceans

Singing songs

That only you understand

There are wild horses running towards

You

Pleading!

Polar bears dying

For one last kiss with life

There are the deep mysterious

Eyes of sacred orangutan

Looking deep

Into your being

Yet

We don't want to look

In their eyes

Extinction

Is not a birthday card

Anyone wants to open

It's not a voucher

To be spent at the till

There are words

Inside you

That have never

Been spoken

That may

Just open

The door to more than a

Survival

That you once dreamt of

Some wild

Odyssey

Will take you

If you let her

Her life

A dream

That you can

Barely remember

Long

Before you were born

You had a wishbone

Made of flesh and feather, scale and

tongue

The silence

Is inviting you to remember

His name

Somewhere inside you

Is pan

Forgotten

Waiting

There is Hermes

Purring

There is sea eagle

Diving

There are coral reefs

So bewildering

Their beauty will break you
Like beauty does
When not understood
Properly
There is a lover
Inside each one of us
Longing To be ravished
By the dawn

Nothing for granted

Isn't it amazing the infinite different faces that make up this world. Each human, each animal, each plant, cloud, water droplet unique in its radiant splendour. As one sits and watches the various flavours, smells and colours of the hustle and bustle of the city, one can not help but be in the wonder of it all. The endless spontaneous majesty of life as it meets the open space before it. How incredible that we are not in control of our thoughts or feelings, they are just forever reacting and responding to a multitude of infinite causes and conditions in each given moment.

Just to be here, witnessing the show, is such a miracle, such a gift, it is almost beyond words the ecstatic wonder of it all. It is too easy to forget the beauty of it all, to curl into a cocoon of self referentiality, to become complacent in the conceptual illusion that we are somehow in control, but worst of all, to think we know who we are.

Our name was given, this mind is ever changing, the display of life unfolding before our eyes is forever in motion, nothing, no matter, how it seems, is ever the same. We can take nothing for granted, literally, we do not know when we will pass from this world, what will happen tomorrow, never mind next year, or even in the very next moment.

Yesterday, my mother who lives in Andalucia, shared some really sad news. A friend of a friends 3 year old daughter was killed whilst waiting to get in the car at a supermarket. A tourist pulled into a parking space, and ran her over, he tested positive for cocaine. The immensity of that moment for everyone involved is incomprehensible. Before we judge and name it, the felt sense of that moment will in some way ricochet across the universe.

We can take nothing for granted, this very moment is all we ever have. If we don't recognise the wonder of being right now, there is no guarantee that we will have another opportunity. It really is that simple. Every moment can be full of wonder, the wind in the trees, a fan whirling, the cacophony of birdsong and rickshaws, sunlight on the water or the call of prayer from the mosque.

And as I sit here watching the endless dynamic movement of it all, it can be heart breaking in its intensity, in its fierce unknowable beauty, to be open to it all, the vast open radiance. No wonder, we want to pull away and hide behind screens, behind beliefs and concepts, behind name and form, behind knowing and judging, naming and labelling, putting everything into little boxes, like the houses we inhabit.

Sometimes, it's good to say "fuck this" and walk out of that box, to just go, to literally take off, not knowing where you will end up that day. I often do this, get in the car and just see where I end up, find a new forest to walk in, explore a new country, try a different class of hotel, eat street food in an obscure backroad in a Delhi, then try a five-star place. Why not? Life is full of wonder, let that wonder become one's song line.

Don't look now!

The night pulls you into her wild
abandoned life
and kisses you with a secret
that has never even been told.

Don't look now,
for you might just become the mystery.

Don't even try to hold on,
Just for one moment be like a galaxy,
stretching her silver laced gown
across the stormy ocean of your heart.

Let go utterly into now.
Wanting no thing,
being no body,
just go back to the beginning,
for there is no end to love.

Wishes call you into dreams.
The fire of your being is,
she who has no name.

When the me has gone,
the I has forgotten,
the we is woven,
the they has forsaken,
the us has dissolved
and only love remains.

Suddenly!

Suddenly the recognition arises, in that
moment, it is obvious it never went away.
The imaginary self seems to have
forgotten its own essence and gets caught
in a myriad web of thoughts and feelings.
The thoughts and feelings seem to bring
confusion or suffering it's in all its
disguises, the sense of self activated or
triggered, into a spiral of self
referentiality.

Yet in those very feelings is either the
cause of suffering
or the very root of freedom.
Whatever that word means.
In this case it means, seeing the very
emptiness of all things
as nothing but the radiant display of
awareness.

For to follow the thought or feelings outwards to an external object, whether that be a person or thing, projections, desires and all the consequences of that trajection, seem to hold the answer.

Whereas, often they are just spinning a web of endless cause and effect, as if we will somehow solve our life crises in the dream or movie we are watching.

Yet of we turn attention back on itself, not to get caught in a process, or another series of concepts or stories about the thought or feeling, but look directly at its very root, then it is obvious, every trigger is an invitation to know one's nature.

For example, a feeling of anger or jealousy, a story of poor me, a script arises in the mind, we can try and sort that out with the object, which if a person, which often at best, just puts a plaster on the wound, until the next time it is activated by a different object or situation.

Yet if we look at its very root, the feeling is arising within consciousness, the object is simply reflecting whatever is arising within awareness, the object/person is not feeling what is arising in this awareness. By recognising the root, that being awareness is where all feelings and thoughts arise, then by resting back in our own essence, which is awareness, which is just another name for space or emptiness.

Not a dead, hollow, black hole, but a vastness that allows all things, it does not judge, nor have any boundary or edge, it is neither good or bad, higher or lower, it does not have a task or intention, it is not superior or inferior, it has no name, no beginning or end, yet all these things arise within this radiant brilliant awareness.

When this is recognised, it is obvious there is only ever awareness or spirit in a dance, effortlessly playing hide and seek, in a dream like illusion. When this is seemingly not recognised, the whole world feels like separate experiences to be dealt with, one after another.

Do we have choice, it may seem so, yet in reality everything is just happening, including this dream like body, with its dream like dreams.

How beautiful the moon

How beautiful the moon,
when no one's watching,
how enchanting the sky,
when midnight dances.

How crazy are we,
grasping for meaning,
have you ever looked?
Because there is no one at home.

How crazy the thieves at midnight,
how wild is the wind in the trees,
I thought I was alone,
but I was only waiting for her longing.

How long is the beginning,
when there is no end.

How many words can we use,
to describe the infinite?

Deja woke up,
drank the wine of love,
and cried tears of grief, at joy!
and this is, how.

It has always been.

Albion

What is it about nature and the wild,
that human beings find so threatening,
Why do we seem to want to destroy our
home and everything in it?

In our lovely highly polite and properly
mannered countryside of Albion we have
pretty much sanitised and destroyed
our wilderness. Anything that can hurt us
or, God forbid, kill us, we have destroyed,
already made extinct here.

Yet we shout from the hallowed pages of
The Daily Mail if other countries choose to
wipe out their ancient forests or destroy
their wild habitat. Yet still under the
illusion of polite society, they hunt and
kill the last few wild creatures we have,
either for fun or profit.

Badgers are culled, because of a very tenuous link. Hen harriers, Buzzards, Red Kites and even Golden Eagles are killed by the gamekeepers that look after the huge estates that make up a large part of the last wilderness on this sceptred isle Most of the land is owned by less than 5% of

the people, and this has pretty much been the same since the Norman invasion: The 7th Duke of Westminster, for example,
recently inherited an estate of around 140,000 acres worth £9 billion. As the previous duke once said, when asked for advice on how young entrepreneurs could succeed: 'Make sure they have an ancestor who was a very close friend of William the Conqueror.'

But it's not just like this in Albion, all across the world human beings are destroying nature. Maybe we are so scared of the wild, like some primordial fear of the unknown, of that which hath monsters, wild animals that can kill us. So by killing them and their b=habitat, we are so mehow safe. That certainly seems to be part of the story here. Any attempt to re-wild the country with anything that is any perceived threat is met with flaming torches and is lost in the bureaucracy of the long hauls of Westminster. Maybe our obsession with lawns, golf courses and shopping malls, is our compulsion to try and control everything, yet somehow

knowing on a much deeper level, m that
we are not really in control of anything,
not even our own thoughts or desires, our
impulses or reactions. We are spinning in
a vast universe, desperately trying to hold
 onto some sense that I am important and
   what I say and do matters. Maybe, by
destroying everything, human beings are
somehow making a statement, that they
are more important?

Or maybe, Siddharta (aka the Buddha) was
right, and the main problem is ignorance.
And from that primordial mis-
understanding the inevitable compulsions
 of greed, aversion, attachment and anger,
weave together a super fucked up
perception of reality that has caused us to
pretty much destroy the very sublime and
exquisite home we live in. We can't be
much more ignorant than that. Yet the
ignorance he talked of, is not just the

general stupidity that we see, like voting
for Trump or thinking Nigel Farage has
your best interest at heart. But the deeper
ignorance of not recognising your true
nature. For to recognise that you are not
and have never ever been separate from
the source of all things and that
everything arises and ceases from the
same extraordinary mystery.
For to recognise this, is surely the
greatest gift of all, and this very
recognition dissolves the need to control
and destroy everything

From one black crow feather,
we make many orchards.
The deepest love
is one with many difficulties.
Someone who avoids those
is not a real lover.
It takes great courage
to do the dance
of the lovers.
A moment comes
when love touches the soul.
Then you must
give up your life.
You have opened
a secret tonight
that is the night itself,
where black,
dervish-outcast crows
dissolve into joy,
gone to fly
with the white falcon.
Rumi

The Quest

The deep green

Ochre moss

Lichen

Lovers

Will

Be bound

To earth

Long after

Your body

Becomes

A home

For the sky

When all this thunder

That men conjure

In their

Brick palaces

Has fallen

To ash

And

Bone

Ivy

Will curl

Her way

Around the gravestones

Of empires

And battleships

Will be sunken

Homes for barracuda

And owls

The names

Of those ever so mighty leaders

Will be dust particles

In vast sunlit deserts

Their legacy

Unknown

To wind

Or stardust

Pulling you in

And out

Like ocean tides

Licking their salt wounds

Listen to that sound

That purrs

Inside
You
It
Has
No preference
For hatred
It only
Wants
You to hear
The ancient stirring
Of green coral
Forests
And the flicker
Of bird wing
Listen to
The sound
Of the rain
Falling inside you
Let sadness
Break
The treaty
You made

With regret

Even

Now

Dare to lose

Every last

Reference point

To normality

Listen to

The flight

Of the deep

Blue swallow

She has

More important

things

to share

Than

Your

Quest

For freedom

Lockdown: Part 1: The Sands of Emptiness

Strange days are here, nothing is what it seems. Everything we take for granted crumbles, like castles made of sand, that so easily fall to the sea.

Eventually!
This tiny, invisible force can bring down the foundations of this seemingly real and solid society in just a few moments. A whole country locked down, the freedom to move from place to place, to do what one normally does, gone. Just like that!

It is the same with the foundations of our self-identity, so easily swept away by the tides of time. We imagine ourselves to be so solid and real.

We imagine our concepts, ideas and beliefs to have a reality, we defend them, project them, weave our very lives around their seemingly real existence

.

Whole empires, both global and our own little dictatorships, built on the sands of emptiness!

Yesterday, I came across a thread where there were people believing that this whole thing is a hoax and doesn't really exist, no one has died. They are just actors and we are all being played. There are various levels to the conspiracies about why and how, yet the mind has no limit to its potential to weave intricate stories. We are boundless in our madness.

For many people this will be a very precarious time. Events get cancelled, trips and holidays are swept away, people get stranded, people die. People panic, mass buying creates shortages, some people can't get the pain killers they need, hospitals become overwhelmed, like dominoes, the impact is vast.

Yet this has as always been below the surface, society, the self-identity is not solid or fixed, they are impermanent like clouds in the sky, and built on flimsy foundations of shared concepts and beliefs. To take refuge in those things is as futile as trying to catch the sky.

The opportunity in these moments is to recognise the only real refuge. The nature of mind itself. That which is ever present, that has witnessed the winds of appearance ever change. That which never gets old, never changes, is vast and boundless, has no edge or beginning, no limit, no judgement, no right or wrong, no fear.

It is that which is the very essence of everything, it matters not what age, how much money you have, your education or how much pasta you have stored in your garage. It is that which watches the whole world arise and cease, time without end. It is that which is aware of these very words. It is the empty space where the words appear.

Maybe this is an opportunity for the whole world to self isolate, to take a deep breath and see what really matters in this fleeting life.

Friendships and kindness, slowing down
and appreciating the beautiful natural
world around us. Maybe it's time for a
wake up to the realisation we all die and
to rush around gathering objects like
crazy magpies is not what is
fundamentally important.

Maybe it's the simple, the
small, the tiniest fragments of time,
that hold the keys to deep happiness in
this very moment.
The only real currency we have is time.

What is it's worth, what is it
that really counts?

As Zen master Suzuki once said

"The most important thing, is to find
out the most important thing'.

Maybe this is the world taking an
almighty deep breath, to look and see what
we truly value in our lives. Or maybe it's
just a time to buy lots of bog paper?

You decide

True Nature

Always remember your true nature
That's the only practice we will ever need
Not who you think you are
Who you think you are will always get
you in trouble

All problems arise from forgetting
your source
From believing the story of the me
With a body a history a future
You are not your future or past
It's all clouds passing by in the sky

There's nothing the ego loves more than
the drama of the story
But it's nonsense
A dream passing by

But who watches the dream
What's the source of the dream
Who am I truly?

That's the only thing that really matters

Once you find out
That your nothing arising as everything
Then what's to lose
And who can lose it

As long as you think there's something
wrong with you
It's going to be a long slog
Get healed feel better
Feel crap again get healed
It's endless and exhausting

But imagine if we spent as much time
Resting in our source
Rather than worrying
About an imagined past or future
What beauty to know your self
What grace what joy what bliss
Even for a moment taste who you are

You will never go back
It will become the most
important thing in life
To taste that which is infinite
It's always here ever present
Lucid clarity, brilliant awareness
It's the light of the world
And you are that

Luminous emptiness
All encompassing love
Shining presence
And you are that
The source of body and mind
Of the whole universe
Of breath and beauty
And you are that

Never forget who you truly are
Even for a moment
Give your life to this
And all will be well

If you seek reality you must set yourself free of all backgrounds, of all cultures, of all patterns of thinking and feeling. Even the idea of being man or woman, or even human should be discarded. The ocean of life contains all, not only humans. So, first of all abandon all self-identification, stop thinking of yourself as such-and-such or so-and-so, this or that. Abandon all self-concern, worry not about your welfare, material or spiritual, abandon every desire, gross or subtle, stop thinking of achievement of any kind. You are complete here and now, you need absolutely nothing.

Nisargadatta

.

Bardo

After sitting in the presence of the body of our good friend John, who passed away yesterday, there is without doubt the clarity that the body is simply a beautiful intelligent vehicle for that which is utterly mysterious and luminous that we call, life.

It is the spark of consciousness, the vitality of awareness that permeates and animates the mystery of being. Awareness has no boundaries and the presence of the individual when freed from the body has the opportunity to return to its source.

In the Tibetan book of Liberation through hearing (Better known as the Tibetan book of the dead in the west), it is said that at the moment of death, and for a few days after there is the most profound opportunity to recognise the luminous light of awareness as nothing but the nature of mind.

It is often described as the great mother awareness, and we as the child of awareness, who at the moment of death is free to return to our source. If we do not recognise this clear light as our very own nature, if our minds aren't clear or are confused, then we continue on the cycle of rebirth.

It seems to me, and let's be clear, I know very little, that as John was very much at ease and peace with dying and very much at ease in life also, having recognised his true nature again and again, that there was a clarity and freedom and even joy in the presence, a complete letting go into freedom.

It is an honour to witness birth, life and death, and each are an opportunity to have immense gratitude for the gift of presence.

To not take any moment for granted, be complacent or forget for one moment that this life is a wonderful gift, and that is to be shared for the benefit of all beings as much as one is able.

Summer

As the rain falls amongst
the summer flowers,
ten thousand tears pour forth
from the eyes of the beloved.

Sometimes, my friend, a deep and
overflowing sadness
overwhelms the river of this form,
it floods the sky of awareness with a
longing,
like the wolf howls for his mate.

I see, that this deep pool,
is not something to be fixed,
or therapised,
or shut down or even accepted.

It is more than that! If you let it do its
thing, it can break you,
in fact, it should break you.

But not in a way, where you want to
escape or run from life,
but embrace the vast ocean of grief, that
helps you fall in love with life.

The heart, is meant to be broken,
from these shards are the great gifts of
remembering,
of the sadness of all that has passed,
of those shimmering ancestors, who gave
you the gift of this life,
who made wild and unbounded sacrifices,
so you can feel those salty ocean waves
fall from your eyes and the sky.

We are not meant to always be happy,
one day,
we all have to say goodbye.
That grief is the road of belonging,
that my friend is the golden treasure of
appreciation and the seed of gratitude,
for everything, yes, every thing!

Let sadness take you, where it needs too.
If you are lucky, it will break you.
But not in a clinical diagnosis of
depression,
as something to be cured or healed.
But as a boat to take you to the
other shore.
To go beyond fragile concept of
belief or meaning.

Deep in the last forests,
there are birds that have never heard of
human language.
They are the songbirds of your soul.
If you listen very carefully amongst the
deep peace of your being,
beyond understanding,
you will hear their call.

Razors edge

I want to stay out here forever
Amongst summer nights
The smell of pine and jasmine
And nightingales purring
A barn owl
Glides across the golden dusk
The evening stars gather
For their nightly love song

Everywhere flowers yearn for the sun
Whilst the birds lament their passing
A thousand tiny droplets of dew
Gather on the deep green
feathered horizon

A sparrow hawk
Swoops down on the mighty buzzard
A flash of green!
Life in its amazing beauty
If you can't see this
Your eyes are shattered by death

Whilst you are

Barely born

Consumed by concepts

You may as well

Jump now

Why waste all this beauty!

Radiant

Intense

Sublime

A miracle

Not by a god

Or a demon

No need for covered heads

Or crucifixes

To get this moment!

Just this

One taste

Like

Honey

On a razors edge!

The Forest

The forest breathes, it lives, as one. Primordial, intricate, proper wild. Wilder than anything in the mono cultured farmed lands of anywhere I've ever tasted. Wild in its impossible terrain, teeming with life; buzzing, spurting, swaying, humming, dazzling, curling, calling, purring along: like a spell. A dangerous place, untamed, unspoken, non-conceptual, hidden, mysterious in a way that has nothing to do with stories or fairy tales.

This isn't a place for old gods or the new gods, not for Allah or Jesus, or Odin or even Krishna. This is a place before even Pan or Orpheus, before Zeus or Demeter, before Horus or LLud, the sun god. This is a verdant place of life and death forever mingled in an endless cacophony of music, of white-tailed eagles and howling monkeys, of sun bears and tigers, of a billion insects and ants that will eat your soul and think nothing of it.

Here your offerings are meagre scraps on the dance floor of creation, your prayers are mere rustles on the giant palms, ferns in the palm of a monkey's hand, ready to be dropped from a high cliff, to be lost amongst that ancient song, that has no beginning or end. Here, they say, this place is older than all the forests, 250 million years old, they say this place holds 5% of the whole earths biodiversity, but really it is beyond and before time, it is that which spews us out, reminds us of our insignificance as we hopelessly try and take pictures with our tiny specks of technology, which is a meagre gesture compared to the in and out pulsating breath of this place!

This is truly, a place of wonder, for if you can't feel, be lost and fall in love with wonder here, them my friend, you are destined to a thousand lifetimes of mediocrity and the hell of complaining and moaning about this vital gift of an ecstatic life that pours forth through this passing form. Here there is no rushing from one place to the next, no paying mortgages or Brexit, no politics or arguing about who thinks what, why, how or when.

Here there is no right or wrong. There is nothing but this, alive, calling you towards her, like the most exquisite lover, like all gods rolled into one. In Fact, if you want to call anything god, this is her, beaming, staring, singing right at you. If you are prepared she is daring you to stop, listen, look, see, hear her, let her be you, let her whispers curl up inside the most ancient part of you, the one that knows her intimately, like you have always known her.

This place, this ancient being, cares not for the tiny petty games that are played by humans and their ever so important points of view. The views that could and should and will, if given the chance, destroy this wildness, because it can not understand it, it can not control it, only by destroying that which is beyond both control and the intellect will humans create a world devoid of all organic life, of all sentience, of all beauty, a pastiche world of monotony and shopping, of endless consuming like some ogre that has no end to its sloth and ignorance.

Yet she will be here, long after the games of man have fallen to ashes. Here breathing into the dark soul of your being, your divine longing, that which is most ancient inside you, will recognise her instantly, if you really want to.

Yes here, it is dangerous, it is enchanting and inviting, simply because of its wonder, its ferocious beauty. Its bewildering fragrances and its infinite songs, and possibilities. It is alive, so very alive, this earth, wilder and more beautiful than anything we could ever imagine. Yet it is not separate, it is not an other, it is the reflection of our true nature and that is wonder.!

To not see it, is to forever search high and low in the desert of our longing, looking for water, to quench the thirst of our deepest dreaming. Yet here is an elixir, a balm for the heart, a reminder of what we came from and where we will ultimately return, our roots, our bark, our damp mossy births, our earth laden death.

This is the great circle forever turning, enchanting and haunting us with her ecstatic beauty. Can you hear her? If you listen very quietly on a dark moonless night, you may just hear her breathe.

Khao Sok.

Thailand

2019

Majesty of Being

I will call you by a thousand names
Each one will be more beautiful
than the next
That's how it is
In the majesty of being
Every moment
A grander gesture
Than the one before
There is no end to this madness

You are always looking behind
Aa if the past will help you
Or straining towards a future
That doesn't exist

Even you
Were once young
When nothing mattered
But this moment

Losing that!
You will lose your soul
And end up in a home
For delinquents!

For fuck sake!
If you want to go crazy
At least
Do it in style

Fall in love with everything
Every single dew drop of life
Every single beat of the song
Every single strand of life!

I will call you by a thousand names
Each one will be more beautiful than the
next
That's how it is
In the majesty of being

Who am I?

Travelling in-between, doing and being, where is the coastline, and what is the horizon?

Travelling in-between thought and no thought, where is the edge and where is the destination?

Every day I wake up and cry. This world is a treasure of unknowing, a golden canvas of mystery.

If you can't see this, then your too busy watching the fake news of the mind.

There are a billion ways to pray, each one of them begins with this perfect moment.

If you think politics will save you, then become a prime minister!

If you think you can save the world, then at least remember, you are the world.

In the garden, there are a thousand flowers, longing to kiss the sky.

They never ask, "Who am I"

The Beloved

Love hath no words that can describe that
which is always beyond them.

Lying under the clear frost bitten dark,
the call of blackbird and wren like tiny
fragments of silver dew
stir the coiled body from sleep.

The purring of her form, like the tides of
oceans pulling in and out,
her breathe a wave of life,
so simple, so profound.
I lie awake in this early dawn,
as she sleeps sound,
deep as an earth maiden,
laden in shawls
of woven mountain flower and leaf.

She hath shown me loves depths and for
that these syllables are mere footprints
on the edge of salt sea and raging skies.

For that is the meaning if any is to be
given of these ocean ship bodies in which
we relate.

Like sailors into the midnight ocean we
navigate through the tidal currents,
wild storms and long breathes of
shimmering sunlight
on the edge of a never-ending voyage.
My dreaming of pine forests and summer
nights is woken by her stirring,
a blessing.

Soon it is time to trek high into Avalon to
greet the rising fire that gives us all life.

Once a god, now an object,

like so many of what was once deemed to
be   sacred to a people that were in awe of
the wild and this gift we call life.

As I fall into time I pray the children
know what it is to be loved
and allow that splendour to open up every
last fragment of being,
to not turn and hide amongst the pressures
to be lowly and feel less than they are.

For in truth our bones are made from sky,
star sun and moon.

The Ocean Song of Freya

The ocean song of Freya wakes me.
The curling morning mists wrap her silver
cloaks around the ice maiden mountains.
Slivers of sunlight, like shards of sword
and spear cut through the air.

If you close your eyes, you can almost
hear the slice of wooden oar caress the
sea salt,
of warriors coming home from voyages
across the gates of Valhalla and beyond.

There is a sign here saying
"We are travellers"
and indeed, we all are,
whether we know it or not.

Our roots are nomadic,
our soul is endlessly searching and
yearning for new pastures,
for that moment when you first
set eyes on a new land
and you are taken in by
its freshness and wonder
before the clouds of complacency and
habit that obscure beauty with concepts.

A curlew calls on the shining fjords this
morning, such beauty in simplicity.
I share with the children how our English
weekdays are named after the Norse gods
of old, everything is so intimately
connected.

Gone like a flash of lightning are the
white snow deserts of Abisko
with their flaming green aurora,
where the ancient tales of reindeer flying
across the night sky,

have brought the whole world a glimpse
of an ancient shamanic culture, whether
we know it or not.

The Saami have at least
a thousand names for snow.
Yet just like the Navajo, the Cheyenne,
the Celts or the Hopi,
the Saami people have been pushed
further into oblivion,
where now stand desolate mines
and wind-swept churches,
a remnant of a Middle eastern god t
hat offers salvation.

The way the new religion
tried to curve the old,
was through destroying and
burning the drum,
the beating heart of the community,
that helped the people travel through the
great songlines of the mind,

of the spirit world,
of the deep intuitive
language of the earth
that once all people knew.
In that world view,
everything is sacred,
everything has its place.

Norway. 2016

Thirst

This morning the mist curled around the hills like some wild dragon through the pines. The silence is deep, timeless, vast. Swimming amongst these shimmering flowers, four crows fly high and dance along the waves of the sky. Seeing that this whole world is a reflection of what the Sufis call the beloved.

Each face a meeting with every possibility, every conceivable and inconceivable potential.

The smile of a child, laughter, tears, judgement, suspicion, grief, joy, the ten thousand faces of the beloved, ever reflecting and dancing with life.

When perceiver and perceived, subject
and object are no longer isolated,
separated from this unique moment, the
heart is torn open with what can be
described as love.

Any ideas of being different, above or
below, right or wrong, better or worse
are futile and lost in this kind of ocean.
Yet the mind can't help but judge,
compare, create walls of this and that.
Like some kind of ancient rusty wheel
turning, wanting to know, to feel in
control, to feel all powerful.

You can almost see the mind falling
into its familiar patterns, feeling
comfortable and stable in its perceived
separation. Grasping onto the familiar,
for some kind of recognition that
I exist.

Awareness is the opposite to this machine-like mind, it's unfathomable, unknowable, boundless and vast. Everything is invited, the whole universe expanding and ever changing in its infinite forms, all appearing endlessly like some insatiable dance.

Yet all the while awareness, presence, seeing, is ever present reflecting the whole vast display. There is no beginning or end here, just simply silence watching its infinite potential, no judgement, no commentary, no morals, just being, simply being.

Yet words can never do this justice, they are incapable and limited by the mind that makes and creates them.

Words themselves create a separation as the mind's cogs try desperately to understand, decipher and make meaning.

But what does this moment mean?

In the end only love remains, a love for this moment, this delicious moment we call life.

Wedding night- An ode to Rumi

Do not be sad on my wedding night,
For now, I shall be married to eternity
When I was hidden in the darkness
of the womb,
How could I bear this light of being?

When I stumbled my way into this form,
How could I have ever known,
The silk pearls of her lips,
The beauty of the beloved's embrace.

As I lay in that ocean of becoming,
And a whisper had told me,
of the high snowy mountains,
The vast desert sands,
The kiss of the rain, the clarity of night

Would I have believed,
just one word spoken?

How can there be an end,
to that which has no beginning,
how can I cry to lose,
that which I never owned.

This fear of death,
is it not a fear of the unknown?
Who knows, what lies behind,
this rose garland curtain?

Do not be sad on my wedding night,
as finally I get to meet myself.
When I spent my whole life,
searching for,
that which has,
always been on my lips.

Do not wander,
alone and longing.
Searching for a treasure,
you have never even lost.

A flame of love,
has burnt this self into ashes.
In your presence, beloved,
I am no thing, yet everything.

Do not be sad on my wedding night,
I am so happy,
I can't stop these tears
The grief of knowing you,
has taken me home,
to the centre of the heart.

Do not be sad on my wedding night...

Hiraeth

Hiraeth: A welsh word that more or less means a deep longing for home.
For a while now I've been meaning to travel back to Snowdonia and Ynys Mon (Anglesey), where I grew up. Home of the ancient druid priest and daubed women warrior that shook fear into the Roman legions. It may not seem like an epic adventure, like travelling to the mighty Himalayas or trekking across the wilds of Patagonia, yet it has its own wildness, its own distinctive allure, especially when there's the opportunity to see old friends, one hasn't seen for many years, plus close friends pilgrimaging there from Cumbria and even more rare, a May forecast of perfect weather.

As human beings we have a tendency to forget, to constantly recoil in a collective amnesia of what's most important in life. The daily complacence can swallow us up in the small details and forget the bigger picture, to forget to re-member - literally come back together.

Sometimes a force beyond the conceptual mind, pulls you towards an unknown metaphor, a secret that the body knows, but the mind is far to intelligent to re-call.

And it's only when it's least expected, that the mystery unravels itself, a moment of Ah Ha!
Much as I love the cottage garden houses, domesticated fields and well-managed woodlands of Sussex and Southern England, there is nothing quite

like the ruggedness of the boulder clad mountains that greet you on the journey to Cymru. Once you have driven up the motorway and monotoned urban landscape of Birmingham, the conformity of Telford and the rolling hills of Shrewsbury, you literally step into another land.

Yes you can take the motorway all the way if you like, or you can take the long winding road through forested valleys and glades, rolling rivers and old slate houses, where petrol stations aren't run by BP but some old gimmer, where you wonder if the pumps still work, as they are covered in rust and in the tiny shop foyer, a latte has yet to be discovered.

Instead you step back into a timeless place, for me a conjuring of memories, a journey as a child that would be taken maybe once or twice a year, to visit the big cities, where they had big shops, with big names and things like theatres and decent football teams. As a kid, Chester was an adventure, London was the capital of the world. We went there to go shopping, to see the lights, to marvel at the wonders of Oxford street and the hallowed roads of Carnaby.

But this was another kind of journey, a stepping back, a re-winding up thot ancient pathway of horse drawn carriage and pilgrimage. This was the land of Eagle once, Snowdon's name in Welsh is Eryri or Eagle! Now there are no eagles as such, but red kites and buzzards, otters, and seals, porpoise and stone chat, merlin and sparrow hawk.

It feels good to see old friends, sea captains and butchers, taxi drivers and fishermen. This is not the place for tantric workshops and Satsang's, no one is trying to sell me their spiritual prowess or follow the latest guru. (btw there is nothing wrong with that, it's just something else.).

Here people seem to be made of rock and stone, of sea foam and oak, of laughter and life as it is. There is a closeness to the land, a simplicity that I love. There is no pretention of enlightenment. Yes, there are the challenges of life, there are those that never escaped and those that never needed to.

Yet most of all, I realise this place is in the bones, it has roots inside me. Yes, we are but particles of dust, woven by emptiness, but we also have the rivers and mountains of feelings, of earth, of lust and desire, of grief and longing, we have the ancient tales of the Mabinogion, living inside us. The Mabinogion being the oldest written stories of Britain that are woven in these lands and point to that which is beyond the daily grind, in a language that is both archetypal and epic in its timelessness.

As I arrived along the coastline of the Menai straits I passed the small house, overlooking the sea and Anglesey, that my Nain and Taid (Grandparents in English), lived in all their lives. I would visit them nearly every weekend and sit down with my grandfather as he told me tales of how he went to school with John Wayne as we watched his movies, and his tales of being in the merchant navy, whilst my grandmother cooked dinners that looked much like those mountains, piled up, like rocky outcrops, each thing piled on top of each other.

And as I passed by, I felt a deep grief in my body, that they were no longer there and I couldn't pop in, to tell them about their great grandchildren and the weird wonderful places I have visited or the people I have met on the way. Yet that night, staying at one of my oldest friends, Tiger's house, I awoke in the middle of the night, I vowed to visit their grave, where they are all buried, with my dad and his brother.
And I remembered that in Tibet, in Asia and many places across the world, it is normal to have a spirit house on your land and to each day feed the gods and ancestors (in Thailand they like cake and Fanta apparently, as the ancestors

have sweet tooth's).Partly to remember, but also to partly wish them well and to make sure they do not haunt you with their ancestral patterns that they themselves may not have released. And I saw in our graveyards they are like deserts, often just lines of gravestones, with no flowers or food or remembering, apart from maybe those that have died recently and those that maybe live nearby, may occasionally bring some flowers. And that's just the last generation, who remembers the great grandparents?

Who even remembers their names or where their graves are?

We forget, we become forgotten.

Our lives just tiny fragments of dust in the great mystery of being.

So, I decided to feed them and wish them well and bless them. I found a branch of kwik save, an ancient shop, long before the modern temples of Waitrose and Lidl. This is where my Nain used to go. I lay at their grave some potted flowers, so they may last, a Swiss roll, a scotch egg, a bar of fruit and nut, a Guinness and 4 fags, because they all loved the odd fag.

I lite some Tibetan incense, did the appropriate offerings and left them happy I hope., Maybe it's pointless like all gestures, empty, without meaning, but that is the beauty of emptiness, it's a free for all, you make your own meaning,

I visited my ancient child hood home, once a place to the Princes of Gwynedd, then a home to a lord, then a broken monastery before later becoming a brilliant hotel, where I once lived. It is a beautiful place in May, surrounded by ancient woodlands, with views to Snowdonia over the straits.

Yet I was glad to leave when we did, as it meant my mother could live and be the inspiration she is today. Now it is a snobby time-share for golfers and that is the way of the world, hence the rise of Donald Trump.

Ynys Mon is stunning in good weather in May, the tiny roads with the flowering byways, the shimmering sea, the wildlife and memories of being a child before computers and day time television, each turn in the road held a memory, of bunking off school, of courting and the first kiss, of ancient hidden mansions deep in the forest

Overgrown temples to the wild, of ice creams and sailing, of jumping off the pier and swimming in the sea at summer, of fishing for mackerel or the long summer holidays, where we only ever go home for tea and then be out till the late summer sun sets.

Of denim jackets and AC/DC blasting on the radio, of pretending to be Indians in the forest for hours, familiar amongst red squirrels and endless wild garlic glades, of death slides and grifters, of 99 flakes and scampi in the basket. Beautiful days, halcyon days, sublime memories, all like fragments of dust in the vast empty sky!

And now after 8 hours journey, I have ancestral lag, exhausted and happy to re-member and be home

The Feast

Oh, bearer of secrets,
you whose cup is always empty but full,
bring me a cup of your essence,
so I may drown in love.

Tear me away from concepts and dreams,
of finding you somewhere else,
have you not heard dear wayfarers,
that god is in your kitchen.

Yes, she's cooking up a right old feast,
from the bones of your personality,
your nice smiling face,
looks good in that sacred soup.

Yes, gather round the dinner table,
for god is preparing a feast so vast,
that there is no end,
to its delicacies.

Look at the menu of life,
and choose the finest dish,
those subtle unborn flavours,
are bound to stir your soul.

For the first course,
It's your concepts,
you'll need a fish knife,
to pick out those stale bones.
For the next course,
its beliefs,
no room for vegans,
when picking through those fleshy
tones.

Now for the main course,
ah, yes, it's all about me,
you'll need a big appetite,
to polish that one off.

Let's take a moment,
to taste the fragrance,
of gods delightful meal,
it's been brewing since eternity.

She's been busy making
all kinds of dishes,
yet you turn away with allergies,
I'm not surprised you cannot eat,
all that beauty is a lot to stomach.

But, listen, gods cooking up
a big old feast,
and invited you to the table,
just try one taste,
and you'll never be the same.

Did you know that every single recipe,
from this kitchen,
was made by the sun,
deep in the fire of your soul.

Can you ever even begin to imagine,
how long she's been cooking,
yet you're too busy looking,
at the ingredients.

Every single heart fire
that has ever been lit,
was only for you,
to taste,
this delicious feast.

But there you go,
wandering from one
restaurant to another,
searching for that perfect meal,
which has always been on your lips.

For words are like god's food,
sweet and sour,
bitter and spicy,
sometimes hard to swallow.

Why not have a glass of wine,
with your meal
it may loosen up the bowels
to talk more gibberish.

It's time for the sweet trolley,
what will you have
a trifle more indulgence
of the self.

Why not try,
a slice of love,
it may just break open;
that aching heart.

Come friends and family,
gather around,
for gods having a feast
and you're always invited!

Form is emptiness, Emptiness is form.

Heart Sutra

In order to truly know one self and live to one's highest potential then maybe there is a calling for a deep integration of both a direct realisation of the sublime clarity of non-duality, along with the compassionate wisdom of form.

To understand our non-dual nature, one simply turns one's attention from that perceived to the actual perceiver, directly looking into the nature of mind, one realises that there is no independent self, but rather a continuous sense of self that feels permanent but in reality is ever changing in relation to circumstance. Our minds nature is awareness, which is the mirror that reflects the ever-changing self.

Yet we live in a world of causes and conditions, of form and emptiness. Knowing one's nature is awareness, does not stop one being an arse from time to time. One only has to look at the ongoing catalogue of teachers who continue to create suffering whilst denying their shadows.

Our body is form. Form includes our conditioning, by culture, family, habits, addictions, neurosis, it is bound to cause all sorts of anxiety, it is simply the sacrifice of having this body. Form is the exquisite vehicle that allows us to experience this vast, beautiful world.

Yet by bringing the clarity of awareness to the conditioning of the body and all its intimate and intricate weavings, one can slowly be free of the patterns that

sabotage our potential, to open deeper
into the mystery of being itself.

To try and live our wildest dreaming
without continuously bringing our deepest
awareness to both form and emptiness, is
like a hamster spinning in the wheel.

Hey fool!

Hey fool!
Curling up inside
The tomb
Of whispering thoughts
Surely
It would be better
That you
Lost your mind
Than gathering
All that dust
Of separation
Between your ears
The deep green
Ochre moss
Lichen
Lovers
Will
Be bound
To earth
Long after

Your body

Becomes

A home

For the sky

When all this thunder

That men conjure

In their

Brick palaces

Has fallen

To ash

And

Bone

Ivy

Will curl

Her way

Around the gravestones

Of empires

And battleships

Will be sunken

Homes for barracuda

And owls

The names

Of those ever so mighty leaders

Will be dust particles

In vast sunlit deserts

Their legacy

Unknown

To wind

Or stardust

Pulling you in

And out

Like ocean tides

Licking their salt wounds

Listen to that sound

That purrs

Inside

You

It

Has

No preference

For hatred

It only

Wants

You to hear

The ancient stirring

Of green coral

Forests

And the flicker

Of bird wing

Listen to

The sound

Of the rain

Falling inside you

Let sadness

Break

The bond

You made with regret

Dare to lose

Every last

Reference point

To normality

Listen to the flight

Of the deep blue swallow

She has

More important
Prayers
To share
Than
Your
Quest
For freedom

Roaring Emptiness

The immensity of silence
It's roar
A thousand waves
Pounding the sky

With beauty!

Sea birds and crows
Gather
By her
Deep blue

Rivers
Edge their way
To her
Gateway

Bringing
All thoughts
To thunderous
Nothing

The mighty

Gods

Of sun and earth

Are her bone quilt

Tearing

Away

The webs

Of monotony

Of despair

And the meaningless

Tides

Of presumption

Here

There

Is only

Breathe

After breathe

Beautiful Moon

It's a beautiful moon tonight

But don't rely on astrology

To see her

face

Every star

Has a secret message

But no one

Can tell you

What that is

It's only

Direct

Experience

That can unwind

The revelation

Of

What is

Soothsayers are unemployed
In the majesty
Of this moment

The beauty
Of just this
Is the divine
Truth

For truth
Is only
This moment

No one can give
You this
No matter
What
You believe

God and nations
Are the most
Intricate
Concepts

People
Give
Their lives
To them

Yet if u look
At that
Which is aware
Of everything

Quite
Easily
You find
The holy grail

Quite simply
Relax
With no thing
To do
Or be

No stress
Or anxiety
Or grasping
Or need

Everything
Is
As it
Is

Perfect

Whispers of Midnight
(A Song for Caburn).

The stars have flooded the sky,

as midnight whispers moonlit,

& sweet tears of the beloved have

gathered,

at the heart of your being, my love.

Silence rushes her dark curls,

upon your lips, my heart,

& galaxies have been burnt,

in your eternal presence, my love.

Everywhere & nowhere they gather,

at your grave,

to sing laments at your beauty,

to hear the cries of your soul, my love.

Turning this way & that,

searching high & low,

for some spark of embrace,
with your eternal secret, my love.

How the sunlight dances on your ocean,
and the wind cries your promises,
but who is listening, my beloved,
who is listening, my love.

The dawn has gathered on your sky,
her dress laden with gold,
her mermaid's tears, beckoning,
for one last kiss of life, my love.

Summer, twists and turns in her shade,
the green velvet meadows sing her lament,
crescent birds fly high, leaving no trace,
as your luminous mind shines, my love.

Twilight sings a love song,
trees are humming that olde sacred tune,
but who is listening to your whispers,
who knows the words, my love.

Deep amongst your burning pyres,
where whole worlds are born & unborn,
where only sacred lips taste the day,
there's a prayer made of stone & shells,
my love.

If only I could speak one word,
to bring you to this shrine, my heart,
I would sing it high from the hill,
where promises have dropped from our
eyes, my love.

There's all kinds of clouds this morning,
holy ones & thunder beings,
they've come to gather upon your shore,
& offer you our salt lake tears, my love.

Oh beloved,
you who has no name, no form,
yet arises as this sacred dance,
take these prayers of beauty, my love.

Never, shall I look for you,
amongst the dark corners of concepts,
never my sweet, shall I search for you,
amongst that funeral of beliefs, my love.

You who has arisen in my heart,
as this vast and ancient beauty, earth,
I shall never stop dreaming of you,
Oh beloved, my heart, my soul, my love.

Lewes. Sussex.

24th June 2011

Live and die without regret

The golden moon rises through the night sky, showing her majesty through the scattered clouds over Bera island. A thousand or more stars caress the sky above the fierce roaring Atlantic below. The crash of wave, pounding crag and sea salt woven black molten temples lie bare to the mighty elements.

Each moment flickering to the next, hail thunder, snow, frost, sun, warmth, radiant clarity, torrential rain, rainbows, swirling storm clouds, villages battered down to the green peat where ancient forests once stood, hanging on like lichens to the edge of the land. 10 houses, 4 pubs, a barren tune on a windswept wedding.

Here high above the ocean, the fire crackles, just the breath and flickering candle. Stillness, stretched beyond time and space, neither inner or outer, one taste, where all things arise and cease in an endless dance of the elements.

It is only when one reaches the silent wild places, one sees how truly exhausting life can be. We barely take a moment to truly stop and take stock, to see how we got to where we are right now. Bombarded by constant adverts, images, pulls and pushes, life seems to propel us into one imaginary decision after another, pulled by the sway of what society or are particular cultural conditioning sings to us. The farce of social media and its tempestuous prayers to the glorified god of self-identity. Rising up through the Imaginal mantras of the great goddess and gods " insta-gramitius" and "farce-bookitiumeous"...

The stench of anxiety is not dissimilar than the pungent smoke of a lingering cigarette.
In the same way the smell and taste of deep peace lingers mysteriously in the vast open space, how does a place retain a sense of deep peace or stress, when it's fundamentally just forms arising in emptiness?

Throughout time, people and pilgrims have sought retreat, a chance to gather one self and see a wider perspective of this mysterious life. Whether consciously or unconsciously, whether with spiritual intention or not, it's an essential aspect of this being human, to step away from the constant distractions, so we can literally sit in wonder at this precious human life.

Who knows what happens after death, there are infinite beliefs and concepts, but in reality, no one really knows. Maybe this is it, and in many ways, what a great relief if that is so, or maybe we continue to search endlessly for some meaning, for some goal, to find out what the fuck this is all about. Hey, we might as well prepare, there's nothing like turning out in a storm without a jacket and decent footwear!

I think the great Tibetan yogi Milarepa said it best.

"My religion is to live and die without regret."

If there is any practice it is surely this. Yet as human beings we are conditioned and often compelled by our desires and aversions, which manifest in anger, pride, jealousy, lust and ignorance. To shine the light of awareness on our shadows, our own unique conditioning, is both a challenge and a gift. There is no one immune from these aspects, some are more pronounced, but ultimately we all fall prey to these aspects of human nature.

To come on retreat is an opportunity to be honest with oneself, to deeply look at these conditions and re member that we don't need to be too hard on ourselves, that deep love and compassion, along with the vibrant wings of wisdom, are always available.

A good teacher is someone who embodies these qualities and shines a mirror of radiant clarity to our own intrinsic nature, which is nothing but the perfect radiant expression of life itself.

A cat does not feel guilty about killing a mouse, the wind does not care for the rage of a hurricane, the ocean waves have no regrets, life is both exquisitely peaceful and a perfect storm. The question is, can you recognise your own perfection.

The mind, just like nature cares not what I seem to do. Yet what I do, has an impact on being, or rather the recognition of being. So being clear, isn't about a dualistic concept of good or bad, but simply a matter of being with what is and recognising that each paths potential may have different outcomes, one more likely to sabotage awareness of our natural clarity, the other more likely to enhance or support its recognition. Hence, it's compassion and wisdom in action.

Essentially remembering that true bliss is in the being, not in the objects of desire.

Cake is nice, but it doesn't block awareness, unless you eat so much that you dislike your form and it becomes obsessive, it's all about balance. And one has to know one's ability to balance certain elements, we all have our own triggers. Taking a step aware from the compulsive and familiar truly is a re treat, a gift to oneself, to be with the actuality of being, away from the constant stimuli of repetition.

My advice, for what it's worth, go to some wild beautiful place every now and then, don't go on the internet or phone anyone, whilst your there, forget the news, radio, emails, newspapers, even books, just be where you are. Whether it's an afternoon, a day, weekend or month. (There's nothing inherently wrong with any of these things, they all have their uses, it can also be a great relief to have a break from them.)

Stay with the sense of "I" above all.
Anything after, such as I am this or that,
let it dissolve like clouds in the vast open
sky, just returning again and again to the
simple feeling of being. What becomes
obvious is the natural world is truly
radiant, full of wonder, surprises,
incredible displays of light and beauty,
ever changing, fresh and spontaneous and
you are that!

Dzogchen Beara. Beara Peninsula. Ireland.
Full Moon. Jan 2018

The Deep Blue

Bats fly high

Through

The deep

Blue

A thousand

Poppies

Gather

To kiss the sky

I remember

You

By the whispering

Winds

By the holy dawn

The swirling

River

The contours of birds

The echo

Of dawn

The twilight

Of the candles flicker

The skylark

Song

The great

Wild moon

Mostly

I hear

Your

Laughter

Through

The roaring

Mind

And it's waves

That lash

Against

The hearts

Shore

I remember

You

With the tears

Of rain

Falling

Like prayers

On the deep
Green earth
Our longing
Is like
A blanket
That threads
It's beauty
Across
The stars
Weaving
Songlines
Between
This world
And yours
I hear you
When
Everything
Stops
Silence
Beyond
Words
Just

Like
This
Our
Lives
Are
A
Shimmering
Crown
Of
Lovers
Yearning
For
A
Kiss
With
Emptiness
Just
Like
This!

Song for a broken heart

All I have to offer you are my tears,
please take these salty lakes and go,
I turned and ran into an ancient forest
glade,
and sat under this cobweb of stars.

I can hardly bare this love,
she haunts me night and day with her
beauty,
she has ravished me by her tears,
and still she has not kissed my lips.

I used to dream that I was separate from
her gaze,
now I know, it has broke my heart,
how could I ever forget,
this ancient longing.

Flames rise from ashes,

her smile flickers on the ocean of my
soul,
utterly grief ridden by love,
I try hopelessly to walk home.

Just as I have given up every last shard
of hope,
she kisses me and I die a thousand
deaths,
I swear I will never turn my back,
and abandon her again.

Fool! she cries,
by night you will have forgotten,
and desperate in your amnesia,
you will look everywhere for me.

Whilst I, will be sleeping,
in the pieces of your broken heart.

<u>I used to be Buddhist, now I am a free man...</u>

<u>Taxi driver</u>
<u>Colombo</u>

As we swirl in and out between bus and rickshaw on the winding lush mountain roads between Colombo and Kandy, our taxi driver spurts out pearls of wisdom spontaneously, amused by everything, seemingly in love with his job and life.

A far cry from the hustle and bustle of the temple of the scared tooth, where every pilgrim this side of Kailash has crushed into the puja to get a glance or even better there's prayers being answered.

As I'm shoved along in a throng of people, grasping onto some object in the hope that they have a baby, get a new car,

win the lottery or find a decent girlfriend,
I can't help but feel an overwhelming
aversion to religion and think of the taxi
man driving up and down the hills
chucking to himself.

Why do humans feel the need to look
outside themselves for peace of mind, for
happiness. Buddha asked for no images to
be made of him, it is said and not for his
image to be worshipped and prayed to but
follow his teaching. Yet the taxi driver
said, no one meditates, they pray and
worship and offer flowers and money in
the hope f done boon, certainly not
nirvana which would mean giving up all
this stuff.

Yet there is a deep peace in this place
once the crowd dies away and just the
drums of the monks and piercing long
horns drone their primordial mantras.

And for a moment, aversion passes and compassion arises, for behind human beings grasping is inevitably a longing for connection, for Love, for health and happiness. These things we can never take for granted, so I make an offering, anyway, that all may be at ease.

And off we go with another taxi driver, to see the giant trees, and walk around the lake, where a kingfisher sits silently watching the sunlight on the dappled waves and all is well.

All is well.

Wonder!

Have you ever wondered,
How it must feel,
For a blind soul,
To see?

Have you ever thought,
How it is,
For a refugee,
To find a home?

Have you ever wondered?
How it must be,
For a prisoner,
To be set free?

Have you ever pondered,
What it's like,
To taste,
The sky?

Have you ever felt,

The warm breeze,

Across,

Your lips?

Have you ever dived,

Amongst coral reefs,

And almost drowned,

With that beauty?

Have you ever,

Let silence,

Taken you,

To the source?

Today I heard,

Someone complaining,

Of the state of things.

Yet she had eyes that see,

And legs that walk,

And a tongue that tastes,

And a wild sunset welcoming her home.

Walking amongst emptiness,
Forever displaying her mysterious beauty,
Roaring with presence,
I bow down in gratitude...

A s   I t   I s !

The deepest joy, the sublime bliss does
not actually come
from a sense of achievement or sexual
pleasure or getting high or from making
lots of money,
But is actually fully available right here
now in this present moment.

Simply sitting and being with what is,
resting in the silence, the empty space
before it is filled with the stories of who
I think I am.

The word "Meditation" or even
"mindfulness" can be challenging
because like every word it has adopted
certain concepts
and ideas of what people think it is.

How difficult it might be or even its
connotation with the word enlightenment
and how there is a sense of purpose or
achievement involved.

Yet in simply being, there is no
achievement, no sense of doing anything
right or wrong, in fact there is nothing to
do at all.

Just be aware of everything that arises in
each moment and simply relax deeper and
deeper into that sense of awareness itself.

Not a sleepy relaxation but an alert awake
vivid brilliant clarity,
that is one's natural state.

Simply allow everything to arise and pass.
Let sounds arise, thoughts arise,
feelings arise all in this vast open
awareness, neither inside or outside.

Neither good or bad, just allowing
everything to be as it is.
There is nothing to control, no one to be,
no where else to be.
Just right here now!

This supreme remedy can cure stress,
anxiety, depression,
arrogance stupidity, boredom, excitement,
lust, anger, angst and any of the myriad
Sensations that arise from this complex
body.
Here right now in being as it is, is
perfection,
is immense beauty, is deep happiness.

It costs nothing and is going nowhere, it
simply is, as it is....

Evening Song

This evening a song was written,
a song of the night,
a dream of midnight,
a star filled galaxy of wonder.

Tonight I am ravaged by love,
god came knocking on my window,
praising my lips with words,
I can barely remember.

When this magic comes to you,
don't wait for wind horses,
to make prayers to the shrine,
that lives in your heart.

Take words and make love,
take your being to the stars,
take your knowing to the graveyard,
and write a song for the evening.

Don't you know,
that everything,
that everything,
is saying, wake up to love!

Don't look back at memories,
they are as unreliable as promises,
they're worse than losing,
the pearl rimmed kisses of your wild
soul.

Go and lose yourself in love,
dare to fall from mountains of pride,
dare to lose your reputation as someone,
write a love song to the midnight.

In samadhi, there is only the feeling

'I am'.

See to whom the trouble is.

It is to the 'I-thought'.

Hold it.

Then the other thoughts vanish.

When these thoughts are dispelled,
remain in the state of meditation.

.

Ramana Maharshi

The splendour of dawn,

The splendour of dawn,
Wraps her misted cloak,
Around this juniper boned,
Wild rose laden sky body.

A thousand feathered tongues,
Bow to dawns curling lips,
Wind horses gather,
Where sky meets sky!

Foxgloves and ferns yearn,
For that which is unborn,
The whole world a prayer,
Of emptiness.

Seeking nothing,
Birds fly,
through open space,
Leaving no trace,

Just like thoughts,
In the vast,
boundless beauty,
Of just this!

<u>Choo Choo!</u>
On a train
Surrounded
By screens
Shields or swords

No One
Looks
In
Your eyes

If They do
It's
Shock
And Awe

Friendly
Fire
Casualties
In the war

For presence.

Maybe
I have
A chip
On my shoulder

Or a thousand
Gratitudes
For
Connection

I stop
And sigh
Swallowing
The whole universe

It's perfect
In
It's
Reminder

Winter

Come,

Let's gather,

all the fragments,

of beauty,

that we have stored,

for the winter.

And

and offer them,

to the sun and moon,

as a gift,

for those moments,

that broke,

open our longing.

When finally,

we saw,

that we are all,

so intimately,

connected,

Like the roots of a forest,

whose woven song,

gives home,

to jaguars,

and golden toucans.

And we,

knew,

that everything,

is just,

a taste,

on the lips,

of the beloveds,

fragrance.

Come,

lets give our,

self,

completely!

You know,
that treasure,
in our chest,
that we keep so guarded,

But now,
is the season,
for giving,
so let's abandon,
the walls,

<u>The scent of mystery</u>
For a moment,
I thought you might,
Remember,
The fragments of your being,
That makes up the sky...

Your holy limbs,
That are woven branches,
That drink up,
Both the earth,
And ocean...

Your wild lips,
That tasted the salt,
A tongue,
That once,
Opened the moon...

Those delicate,
Tiny eyes,
That sing strange songs,

When stars,
Implode your life...

Your soft feet,
That are truly forests,
Where toucans and jaguars,
Leap,
To your knees...

Your broad shoulders,
Hold the whole world,
Closer,
To,
Your heart...

Oh, your open hands,
Are like deserts,
Longing,
For her,
Watery soul...

Your eyebrows,
Are rivers,
That whispers,
To the blood,
That flows in waves...

For a moment,
One brief moment,
Remember...

The scent of your mystery

Shells

I have come to Break

that bond

You made with sorrow

That pulls you under

Like shells to sand

Which somehow

Compels you

To forget

You are a wave

In this boundless ocean

Instead

You get pulled

By tides

As if your

All alone waiting

For the sky
To take you
Home
Again

What madness
Came upon you
To doubt
The secret longing
Of the moon

Whose beauty is
Both empty and form
For without the dark
How would we ever know
The beauty of light

Without tears
How would
We ever
Taste the salt
Of the oceans longing

Nothing, my friend
Is broken
It's just a matter
Of different
Shades of light

In the forest
There are a thousand
Song birds
Forever
Calling your name

How do I know?

I listen to the dawn
Cracking
The world
Open
With silence

5 am

Its 5 am, and I can't sleep,
because the universe is singing a love
song,
so enchanting,
I can only weep.
I awoke to liquid words,
drunk on grief,
clarity dawns,
on this vagabond.
She has shown me beauty,
where meaning drowns,
tears of joy fall like wind arrows

I can barely look in her eyes.
5am,
the sky is a deep blue,
and a fiery blanket kisses the horizon,
an illusion of boundary.

We are never alone,
and never in control,
just dreaming we are,
wake up old man!

She asks us to remember,
please don't forget she cries,

My heart is torn into
ten thousand pieces,
without you.

Listen to the roar of emptiness,
praying on ancient shrines
that you hear, these honeyed words,

Its 5am,
and no one's
sleeping anymore.

Rain

As the rain falls amongst
the summer flowers,
tears pour forth
from the eyes of the beloved.

Sometimes, my friend,
a deep and overflowing sadness
overwhelms the river of this form,
it floods the sky of awareness with a
longing,
like the wolf howls for his mate.

I see, that this deep pool,
is not something to be fixed,
or therapised,
or shut down or even accepted.
It is more than that!

If you let it do its thing,
it can break you, in fact,
it should break you.

But not in a way, where you want to
escape
or run from life,
but embrace the vast ocean of grief,
that helps you fall in love with life.

The heart, is meant to be broken,
from these shards are the great gifts of
remembering,
of the sadness of all that has passed,
of those shimmering ancestors,
who gave you the gift of this life,
who made wild and unbounded
sacrifices,
so you can feel those salty ocean waves
fall from your eyes and the sky.

We are not meant to always be happy,
one day, we all have to say goodbye.

That grief is the road of belonging,
that my friend is the golden
treasure of appreciation
the seed of gratitude,
for everything,
yes,
every
thing!

One, seven, three, five.
What you search for cannot be grasped.
As the night deepens,
the moon brightens over the ocean.
The black dragon's jewel
is found in every wave.
Looking for the moon,
it is here in this wave
and the next.

Xuedou Zongxian, from the Blue Cliff
Record

<u>The tiniest house of time</u>
<u>Sadness: The secret door</u>

Let sadness take you, where it needs too. If you are lucky, it will break you. But not in a clinical diagnosis of depression, as something to be cured or healed. But as a boat to take you to the other shore. To go beyond fragile concept or belief, or meaning.

Deep in the last forests, there are birds that have never heard of human language. They are the songbirds of your soul. If you listen very carefully amongst the deep peace of your being, beyond understanding, you will hear their call.

Just before Phil died last week, in our last conversation he said he wanted to visit Silbury hill and the ancient temples around that area of Wiltshire. I was hoping to drive him there, but it wasn't to be. However, as life and death is mysterious we somehow found ourselves there yesterday. It wasn't planned, we were coming back from a trip and pulled over and there she was, that mighty ancient mound. Summer green and abundant in her splendour.

There is something about those rolling Wessex hills in June, from Avebury to Stonehenge, Pewsey vale to West Kennett, it is a glorious jewel, covered in wild flowers, roaming poppy fields and daisies, buzzards, skylarks, kites and swallows.

Such beautiful blue swallows, diving and dancing in their lapis lazuli enchantment.

It felt like we were being taken to these places, like our dear friend was looking out of these eyes as we sang his old songs and shed both tears for what will never be and joy for what once was.

These places are so old, West Kennett is at least 5500 years old and still the swallows return each summer to that ancient tomb. It was a mere 2500 years later that Christianity became a cult and 3000 when the first Vikings landed to parlay with the Saxons.

This is proper old. It feels it. This is ancestor land going way back.

There is a wonder and depth to these bone stone chambers that bring people back again and again. These most ancient temples to the great mystery of life and death.

For even with our wondrous religions, our glorious science, our holy atheism we still know nothing of death and beyond.

These places remind one of the vastness of it all, like ancient bones left on the earth, to wake us up to the fact that our lives are tiny fragments of dust in the great wheel of time.

We are just passing through like clouds in the vast sky of awareness. Both form and emptiness dancing forever in the tiniest house of time....

<u>Holy Memory!</u>

My

friend

Lets

gather

Your

holy

Memory

Amongst

These

Ancient

Stone

Earthen

Bone

Temples

Like

You

Dreamt

Of

With

Your

Wild

Song

Prayers

Who

Listens

Now

Skylarks

And

Buzzard

Wing

Lovers

Flint

Woven

Tears

Fill

The

Moon

With

Your

Delicious

Longing

There Comes a Time

There comes a time when you start to appreciate the smallest things. The first rays of dawn, the deep silence of that moment as the world awakens. Slowly the birdsong rises and falls like tiny fragments of time being woven together into a blanket of presence so delicate and sublime, it breaks open the heart and mind, if one dares to truly listen.

Above and below the humdrum of news, there is a whole world breathing in and out, pulsating with life, yearning for your glance, longing for a moment with you. She is courting you with her spring flowers and starry nights, her thousand dew drops, the flight of hawk or curling of crow feathers inside you.

Each little thing that we so easily took for granted, now becomes part of our bone woven prayers. Oh to see your face again, the wrinkled smile, the salt tears of your longing for just a moment of tender love. Where the heart opens, the touch of flesh, your beautiful face, a glint of your eyes fire, feeling your fingers wrapped around these old hands as we remember, just remember.

All over the earth, people are looking out from towers praying, for a day when life arrived at their shore, where the fishermen finally came home gathering their nets of love to offer to your hearts temple. Where old grandmothers no longer looked behind them in fear at what may come from that dark unknown.

Where children can play on golden sands, and deep amongst green branches, unhindered by the whispers of adults who hold the doors shut, with love.

A moment where love dogs whine for the moon and the freedom of the open sky. Where we lie together in summer meadows, when night and day last forever, Oh to sit around the sacred table together, drinking the tea and wine of life's sweet beauty.

There comes a time where the world can breathe, can rest, can sit down and cry, for the grief of a thousand lovers is too much for anyone to bare alone. The time has come to weave baskets of a love so deep, as deep as the mysterious ocean, to hold those salt tears that stitch together our longing.

A time to be with the dying and dead, so they know they can never be alone, as long as they live in the temples we have built for them in our hearts.

There comes a time when begin to appreciate the tiniest things.

Enlightenment

Take a moment to hear this wind,
She's pulsating with death
creeping in shadows.

Dreaming of our darkness.
she who births us,
from nothing to being to nothing,
drowning us in emptiness.
smiling at our expectations.

Enlightenment is not a cure,
she says, or a concept,
has nothing to do with success,
it's just a funeral pyre of failures.

I want to hear of your mistakes,
She cries, your burning,
so nothings left.

Deep inside the earth,
Unknown seeds are praying
creating new life,
already kissing the dawn.

Summers wildest kiss has taken me,
She's wrapped me up in her flowers,
and gathered me to dust,
in her cocooned shell.

She's broken my heart to love,
and offered me a glass of life,
which i drank so i could die,
and smile at the milky way.

She's forgotten everything,
Words mean nothing to her,
but still we gather
To offer our salty tears
That once stirred in the ocean
Of our longing.

I'm falling through her heart,
where there's nothing to hold onto,
her pearly eyes are foaming,
her mouth is an ocean of tears.

Her gilded cloak of summers passion,
Has risen,
Now she is adorned,
shining and beautiful.

Fires are being lit,
on mountain tops high above the moon,
the elders are gathering our bones
so we can dream our wildest longing.

Sky Lover, Drum maker

Sky lover, sunset beauty, oracle of laughter, my brother, a thousand bird songs gather, on your horizon, wishing you ease, so graceful, so ecstatic that we will forever dance together in the ashes of being! You my friend are a treasure of all the jewels in the universe entwined... These were our last words with my dear beloved friend Phil. Yesterday he took his last breath, taken to the other shore.

He is one of the reasons me and the beloved met and that gift and meeting him has been one of the greatest of this life. He made the most incredible drums, rattles and ancient ancestral gifts that are reflections of his deep connection with earth mysteries.

We first met 9 years ago when he invited me to a druid festival in Wales. He had bigged me up as some ancient welsh poet, I probably encouraged him at the time, he got me a slot, they were all waiting to meet this ancient relic of Anglesey to lure them to the great bardic paradise of Annwn, but I didn't turn up. I can't remember why, car problems, hangover, probably both in those days.

We didn't speak again until 1 and a half years later, he contacted me about coming to Wildheart, festival the last one. He was with and they set out a sweet stall selling drums. We had lots of fun, he met my dear Tibetan Lama friend and agreed to fix his chod ritual drum 🥁, the one handed down from his ancestors. He did fix it but it got lost in the post, he was gutted.

He then came to the valley of doom, a windswept nightmare of an autumn festival I ran.
We survived but only just.

Then one day in the spring, when I was heartbroken and lost like a raggedy boy making bows from deer bone in the deep forests, I joined in a chat with a young woman he was making a drum with. That's what they did, birthed drums, helped people make their own beautiful drums for life. He was very funny, in fact probably one of if not the funniest beings I have ever met. He was inappropriate, always went too far, had no boundaries. Something I loved after spending time around spiritual folk who somehow thought that wearing white, being vegan, saying the right mantras or following a guru made them special, he cut through all that. Sometimes too far granted, that I wasn't comfortable with, but mostly it was hilarious. So, on this day I joined in this chat about vikings that turned into mankinis and more with Karis. We virtually vibed. Little did I know we would become woven.

Soon after we were courting and one of our first dates was at their Shamtastic drum circles. They were always so vibed. You could properly let loose. It was not a place for the ocd musician or the spirituality retarded, it was beauty, chaos, raw and full of longing. You could properly let go, wail for your loved ones, your grandparents, your ancestors. We stayed with them after, I was still shy, it went well, we were on a journey now, the long boat had left the shore.

Which reminds me, Phil was from York, he was a Viking, with deep roots to this land. He was a wolf brother, he was no sanyassin. We became good friends, we went to Wales together, to the valley of red kites. He got more involved with Into the Wild as it grew, he started running the woodland crafts area.

We went to the Isle of Mull and saw sea eagles, golden eagles, we stayed on the Treshnish peninsula in an amazing cottage. On our last night we saw the most amazing aurora display, it was incredible and on the BBC news next day, a once in a lifetime moment.

He came to James Low retreats and loved Perfect Brilliant Stillness the beautiful audio book on non-duality read by Terence Stamp. He gifted me so many beautiful things, a red deer drum, a Mongolian harp, an eagle's feather, a fire making kit, jays wing, we were always swapping gifts.

Yet he also had a knack of falling out with people and didn't always explain why. This happened with a few folk I know and eventually happened with us. Relationships are strange, they are like oceans, sometimes stormy, sometimes calm, the thing is to remember that we are the wave and the ocean. I won't go into why, what, but just to say much of it he had little choice over, he wasn't in control of his own ship at that point, it was being sailed to another land. We met on a hill by the sea, to say goodbye, I gave him a mammoth bone eagle I had gathered from Navajo lands. We didn't speak for 3 years. He went off to run Roots gathering, it looked great, I would have liked to have gone.

I never gave up. Every now and again I would text. I heard nothing except one New Year's Eve, 2 years in. Just a well-wishing.

Late last year, I texted him again. He texted me straight back and called. So much has gone on. His relationship was over. He was asked to leave the home. He was living alone and was pretty broken hearted plus he hadn't been very well.

He came over for New Year's Eve, he walked in we hugged, it was like we had seen him yesterday. We didn't need to go through a process, we loved each other. We are brothers. We laughed again, we cried, we sang around the fire, broke bread together.

We met up a few times, he wasn't well, then he got diagnosed with pancreatic cancer. We saw him in hospital, luckily Amanda cared for him at first, we went to Catalonia, then suddenly Corona times came. He was dying, a cruel time to go, not being able to see friends, to organise funerals, it was not easy, but he lives each moment, his beauty always shining through. We went to his holy place, Coldrum Stones together before lockdown and he came to our garden before he went to the hospice.

We exchanged gifts, we hugged, we looked in each other's eyes. We said our goodbyes. We both love Phil so much, he will be so missed. His laughter, his brotherly love, I cry just thinking about not sitting together again.

Dear friend may you be free of the pain, the loss, the hardships of the human journey, but may you never be free of the love, the beauty, the joy and laughter of the gods!

May Valhalla's feasting tables be waiting for you with fine mead and warm fires

Here is the last poem of his he shared:

These things that have been crafted by
these wrinkled hands
Float away like soap bubbles on a
gentle breeze
I know not where
their journey will take them

I offer them to the world
So deeply obsessive the art of
construction, the search for perfection
It took me so far from the shore that I
lost sight of the land

Till all I had were the stars to guide me
The moon to sing to
But now I see a new coast line
before me
What strange fruits and creatures
will I encounter

What places of wonder

in the land

of liberation

Wait to be discovered

A falling apart

was just a falling together

A gathering of one's medicine bundle

To dream the dreams

once more

A fresh untainted land

to explore

Mull

Dawn rises over Haunn

A thousand waves

Of silence

Caress the shore

Treshnish opens

To sea eagles

Gathering

Both sky and earth

The old stag

Cruachan

Watches ochre gold

Singing love songs to the moon

Beinn duill

An odyssey

Of stone, bracken

Sea horses cracking open mind

Deep in the rhythm

Of dark earth

the turquoise

Bays of Rubh chaoil call

Golden eagles glide
Effortlessly
Across the sound
Of Creckaig

Once a thousand
Norse warriors
Stood high on Ulva
The Isle of wolves

At Rubha an h-airde
The night sky dances
With the goddess Aurora
On the edge of the world

Mull, fair faced and gentle
One glance
And your lost
For ever

Gathering Dust

Us

Pretentious fools

Think we know

Everything

Our life

Simply

Gathering dust

By the river's edge

We imagine

We know

But we know

Nothing

Like fools

Gold

Intelligent

Idiots

Weighing

Up

Right

And wrong

Twisted

By self made

Concepts

How insane!

You are

Going

To

Die

So why

Waste

Your breath

Debating

This world

Is so

Fucking

Beautiful

But we

Spend

Our lives

In futility

Why not

Bury

Your corpse

Now

It's

Good

For nothing

But compost

Our

Oh so

Intelligent

Reasoning

Has

Brought

This earth

To extinction

Extinct

Your

Beliefs

Relax

Always

There's

Nothing

To prove

An

Invisible

Virus

Can break the chain

There

Is

No

Normal

Just

This

moment

Forever

Give

Your

Self

A break

No one

Is right

Or

Wrong

No one!

<u>Remember</u>

For a moment,

I thought you might,

Remember,

The fragments of your being,

That makes up the sky...

Your holy limbs,

That are woven branches,

That drink up,

Both the earth,

And ocean...

Your wild lips,

That tasted the salt,

A tongue,

That once,

Opened the moon...

Those delicate,

Tiny eyes,

That sing strange songs,

When stars,

Implode your life...

Your soft feet,

That are truly forests,

Where toucans and jaguars,

Leap,

To your knees...

Your broad shoulders,

Hold the whole world,

Closer,

To your heart...

Oh, your open hands,

Are like deserts,

Longing,

For her,

Watery soul...

Your eyebrows,

Are rivers,

That whispers,

To the blood,

That flows in waves...

For a moment,

One brief moment,

You might,

Remember...

Torn into paper flowers

I am torn by your shadow
where you used to lie,
the rose in the garden weeps
for the oak's secret dreams.

The river cries to the ocean,
what more can I say, she sings,
but still you don't look at me,
whilst spring kisses summer.

Nights are cold under this blanket,
the fire of longing has burnt me away,
birds call me home
but no one's listening.

For one moment I saw your face,
in the corner of an eye,
I tried to grasp you,
but there's no one there.

I tore my heart into paper flowers,
and offered it to the moon,
she smiles and said, tell me of love,
embarrassed by her beauty i try to hide.

Always seeking nothing,
nothing seeking always,
behind this veil of thoughts,
a humming bird sings.

<u>Vigil</u>

Each day wakes

With light

A hundred thousand

Shards of light

A silence

So deep

Breaks open

The sky

First

Come

A charm

Of gold finch

Next a raven

Third

An enchantment

Of lupin

Dew

Caresses

Wild

Dog roses

The river

Lapping

Beckons

Kestrel wings

Heron

Calls

Goose

Chicks

To gather

The ashes

Of my dear

Friends bones

From golden

Buttercup

Meadow

To egrets tongue

This time

Is no other time

Either a vigil

Or a loss

A lost

Opportunity

Or a turning

Deep inside you

It's not

Your choice

For if she takes you

You are gone

Like butterflies

On these warm

Spring

Dusk songs

Or for

The lonely

Cues

For fast food burgers

As if

One

Somehow

Missed the call

To take

You deeper

And break

The cracking heart

Inside

you
To
Pieces
For a love
So fiercely
In love
With beauty
Grabs you
And pulls you under
The waves of existence
And that deep grieving lover
That calls your name
On star filled evenings
When there is just you
Alone, but never alone
With just this!
This vigil
That wants
To devour
Your arrogance
Your citadel
Walls

Of wanting

To be right

Of proving

That somehow

You have

Answers

Where

She

The great mystery

Tears your prepared speeches

To pieces

With her

Wildness

Her ravaging wildness

She cares not

For pretty words

For your petty

Sarcasm

Your denial

That burnt

Down the last

Forests

The amnesia

That kills

Your indigenous

Soul

Sit closely

By the fire

Of belonging

Burn

Burn

So

All

That's left

Is

A

hundred

Thousand

Shards

Of

Light!

Drive all blames into one - Atisha

The world of beliefs is as diverse as the universe. Some cry out for freedom, others to stay at home, some say all you need is a healthy immune system, others that it's a false flag, some say this or that drug works, others that it's all a secret plan, some declare it's a police state, others love the impact on the natural world. A vast tapestry of song lines, all permeating through the mind of the perceiver, only seeing the world from that perspective, somehow imagining we share the same perspective, even worse trying to persuade or prove that their view is true and the others is false, like an intellectual battle to prove what exactly?

I am right!

Then what?

Who is this "I" that wants to be right?

Why have we assumed we even know
who or what this I is?

We are so busy investigating fake facts,
we forgot to look at the source of all
this, everything we assume, take for
granted, believe about this me, this I,
this self.

From what I have heard, this corona is a
different for so many people. I know at
least 4 people who have had it, all
healthy folk who have been ill,
exhausted, worn out for 7-8 weeks
ongoing. They are people who eat well,
exercise, are well informed and yet it
has hit them pretty bad. It could be

about to hit the tribes deep in the Amazon, maybe if the soothsayers are right and all you need is a bit of sun and an organic diet they will be fine, or maybe not?

Best not to assume anything and to most of all think about others. If your worried about staying at home is a state crafted way to control you, then you're looking in the wrong place, your true freedom is the other way, look to the ultimate dictator.

If you want to blame anyone or anything, drive all blames into one, the self-cherishing one.

Life is a journey.
Death is a return to earth.
The universe is like an inn.
The passing years are like dust.
Regard this phantom world
as a star at dawn,
a bubble in a stream,
a flash of lightning I
n a summer cloud,
a flickering lamp,
a phantom,
and a dream.

Buddha

Fireflies

Kissing the sky,
swallowing the sun,
this whole world,
a perfect miracle...
who can not see this?
why play with notions,
of this and that,
right or wrong?
maybe there's,
a mystery,
beyond,
that weaved you into being?
who can say?
what this is,
even words,
are just ships
sailing through,
infinite landscapes,
or perceptions,
and wild, infinite possibilities

I have given it all up,

for a kiss with her,

whose heart burns,

even the coldest whisper

i am nothing,

but a swallow,

catching fireflies,

in the sky...

<u>Self-isolation advice:</u>

Truly there is no cause
for you to be
miserable and unhappy.
You yourself impose limitations
on your true nature of infinite being,
And then weep
that you are
but a finite creature.

"Then you take up this
or that spiritual practice
To transcend
the non-existent limitations.
But if your spiritual practice itself
assumes the existence of the
limitations,
How can it help you to transcend them?

Ramana

(Ramana didn't leave his cave for 28 years except for walks, most of that time he barely spoke, yet was beyond happy)

Wild and Golden

The field in the distance is sharp and intense, wild and golden with flowers and the shadows of the pine stands tall like an eternal witness to the rawness of such beauty.

In the distance the geese are calling and the chorus of birds gets ever louder, as if to sing a melody of gratitude to the day for being so full of grace.

Sometimes nature calls to you, like some deep yearning, pulling at those mystical strings of your soul.

The greatness of man's inventions, television, machines, money, grand houses are all laid bare compared to that vastness of nature, its alive, and speaks an ancient language with weather worn symbols, flickering light, dancing shadows and sky like omens.

In the corner of the wide meadow stands an old oak, gnarled and torn by lightning in such a beautiful expression of life greeting death, bluebells gather in groups, where once an old forest had stood, as the sun lowers his gaze and a white, snow white owl shimmers around and around, ignoring our gaze.

A dog barks, the church bells ring, a bee hums, the cool breeze pours through the window and the silence is endless, haunting and enchanting.

Old friends look out of their windows remembering the bonds of life.

A new child, is born in an old cottage,
as the last dying light of rays fall over
the ancient hill, the great miracle of
birth forever pouring forth.

Yet Words can't do justice to life, the
simplicity of the moment, the clear,
still, life pulsating moment...

To know that you are a prisoner of your mind, that you live in an imaginary world of your own creation is the dawn of wisdom

Nisargadatta

Self-isolation advice. Part 2

The eternal optimist

Maybe the greatest conspiracy, the biggest industry, the oldest joke is that people "think" they are, then share their stories with other people who "think" they are, reconfirming each other's self-identity and a world they take to be real and personal. Maybe this is the basis of psychotherapy and 99% of healing/self-help modules.

At a certain level of magnification, the various cells of an organism appear to

be engaged in a fierce and ruthless
battle for individual survival.
Yet if the organism as a whole is
observed at a different level of
magnification, it is clearly seen that
what appears as conflict at the lower
level is indeed harmony at the higher
level.
And so it is with the ceaseless flow of
energy passing through infinitely
diverse patterns, expressing the rhythm
and unity of Life throughout the
changing myriads of forms in the
manifest universe, for which the
illusory individual ego has
unnecessarily and mistakenly assumed
the burden of concern.

Ramesh Balsekar

If you think yourself to be, so you think
the world to be. If you imagine yourself

as separate from the world, the world will appear as separate from you and you will experience desire and fear. I do not see the world as separate from me and so there is nothing for me to desire or fear.

There is no chaos in the world, except the chaos which your mind creates. It is self-created in the sense that at its very centre is the false idea of oneself as a thing different and separate from other things. In reality you are not a thing, nor separate.

While I see the dream as real, I'll suffer being its slave.

Both sleep and waking are misnomers. We are only dreaming. We dream that we are awake, we dream that we are asleep. The three states are only varieties of the dream state. Treating everything as a dream liberates. As long as you give reality to dreams, you are their slave. By imagining that you are born as so-and-so, you become a slave of the so-and-so. The essence of slavery is to imagine yourself to be a process, to have past and future, to have history. In fact, we have no history, we are not a process, we do not develop, nor decay; so see all as a dream and stay out of it.

Shades of Light

Each night I go out to watch the moon
All around are thousands of tiny
boxesWhere people watch other people
On tiny boxes
The sun sets on the oceans edge
Swallows dive deep into the setting sky
Yearning for one last kiss
With this almighty day
Where avatars are born
And someone's heroine dies
A barn owl skims the deep green ve
il Between this world and the
otherworld Dragonflies beckon the full
moon
To pull the tides of ocean breathe
Towards the eternal song
Of life's unyielding ferocious beauty
My lover laments and sings
For the swaying forest
Amongst storm clouds

Her dreaming a prophecy

An exquisite offering

Of her sublime

Being

I write this poem

On a box

Using tiny shapes to make sense

Of the great mystery

Yet the great moon and sun

Arise and fall endlessly

Watching

Empires fall to dust

Nothing my friend

Is important

It's just different

Shades of light

Falling in love with now

Maybe it's the time of year or maybe it's only when things you took for granted disappear that one truly starts to appreciate what is here and now. For me, this spring is extraordinary in its beauty, I can't remember a spring more beautiful. Maybe I say that every year but even if I do there are no complaints.

Maybe it's the slowing down, the no escape to work or achieving, or striving for something. I am just here, and here is beautiful. I can't speak for anyone else because I'm not them, but from awareness here and now, there is a constant stream of gratitude for being alive amongst all this wonder. Ironically, I have not been watching much of the news or movies, but whenever possible, have been out amongst the radiance of nature. For me

this is medicine at its most primordial, there's no need to take anything to enhance it, it is just as it is, ecstatic. Words can't do it justice, everywhere is just bursting forth in some orgasmic kiss with life.
Gary Snyder said
"Become famous for five miles".
Now I truly get this.
Normally I am running around, organising, going into town, having meetings, playing tennis, travelling far and wide, being a bit busy. Don't get me wrong I still have a lot of time compared to many. But a scent of busyness pervades these chambers of being.
Yet now that has changed.
I have spent the last two months exploring the forests, valleys, glades, tides, rivers, beech temples, hawthorn lovers, bluebell choirs, soaring buzzard

baritones, frog rhymes, swan songs, blossoming bonanzas, wild garlic kisses, cherry flower frolics, sweet chestnut whispers, hovering kestrels, majestic sparrow hawked and luscious lupin love poetry in these few miles from my home. This is to name but a few of the miracles that all arise endlessly asking for nothing in return but our attention.

This world may well be "Maya", the great illusion, yet it is an illusion so beautiful and mesmerising in its radiance that there is no end to its majesty.

Today as it happens is the most important festival in Buddhism, known as Wesak and is celebrated annually on the full moon of the ancient lunar month of Vesakha, which usually falls in May.

At Vesak Buddhists commemorate the birth of the Buddha, Siddhattha Gotama, his Enlightenment and his final 'passing' into Nirvana.

What the Buddha realised is that Nirvana is right here, right now possible in this moment. Not in some future moment.

It is the recognition that in this very moment our true nature is awareness.

There is no separation, we are the universe seeing, feeling, being itself.

Buddha gave up his job, self-isolated, turned off the news and sat under a tree, simply being with what is. That simple and direct practice is the same as it was many moons ago, no matter what is going on in the world.

Buddha basically
"fell in love with now"!

Try it, you might never come back!

Swallows

Perfect
radiant
Swallows
Riding
The
Winds of
awareness
Herons
Glide
Beyond
concept
Amongst
A thousand rushes
Croaking

Beyond

name

or story

Frogs

Yearn

For

Love

With their

Divine longing

No beginning

no end

Owls

Swoop

As
All
appearance
arises
and
passes
Like
clouds
in the vast
open
Sky

Natural perfection

takes

no effort

no strain

no manifestation

no doing

no steps

no plan

no problem

It is

as it is

always

already

our

very

essence

<u>Luminosity</u>

Every beautiful garden needs nurturing,
every flower needs water, every ocean
draws in and out. Sometimes the soul
has no choice but to pull you under the
waves, to wake one up from the
enchantment of amnesia that has
swapped a life of valour, of daring or
deep heart breaking love for the false
security of the concrete slabbed lawn,
the four walls of Armageddon, the
peering curtain futility of soul loss and
a numbing that has lost all the flavours
of Neruda or the love sonnets of Lorca,
of the ravishing ecstatic verses of
Hafiz, or even any attempt to truly
understand to what they and all the deep
red roses that we pass by on the street
point to.

It's kind of inevitable that we slip back
into the trackways of habit and forget

our deepest longing. Our whole society
is like a dream machine that peddles out
the mists of illusion that happiness is
something dependent on things.

But why look for happiness, when there
are deeper pools too drink from. Why
with this one precious life, fall back to
sleep and numb out the incredible vast
beauty of it all.
Maybe it's because too fully open to the
vast expanse of our souls calling is to
face all the shadows, the incredible
suffering and pain of existence. To
swallow grief and let it tear us apart, to
dive deep into the roaring waves of
wildness, where no sense of
predictability, no sense of reputation or
even identity holds sway in those
rapturous, havoc foaming sea horses
that will take us deeper and deeper into
what ironically we always yearned for.

When the soul comes knocking you can
try to hide, you can even try to run, but
there will always be consequences and
maybe to actually turn around and face,
(whether you use a mirror or not,
because you don't want to turn into
stone), maybe the best option.

Our deepest nature always wants to be
revealed, to be seen, to be expressed
and when it is, something so unbearable
and beautiful shines forth that there is
no turning back.

You can not forget for long, the
incredible luminosity of being!

For if you do the soul always comes
knocking...

Baboushka

Everywhere on social media are ads or people urging one to do something, to make changes, to be better in some way or another. Courses, conferences with all the best teachers with yet more advice on how you could be better with this endless subtle message and inevitably get some cash out of you to reinforce that they are doing something which they can then maybe pay to do something to think they are also going somewhere. It is indeed a strange old world for humans always the need to do, rarely
simply being.

As for cats however....
The cat wants nothing more
than to rest and occasionally hunt
each morning she watches
the world

There is no idea
of right
or wrong
just the splendour
of life unfolding
She sits
At ease
Watching the world
Go by
Yet she rarely
Kills any being
Never a bird
Or blade of grass
Sometimes
A mouse
Then done
No regret
She just is.
Happy being.
Being!
Be like a cat!

"What has been attained, may again be lost. Only when you realise the true peace - the peace you have never lost - that peace will remain with you, for it was never away. Instead of searching for what you do not have, find out what is it that you have never lost."

Nisargadatta

<u>Akong</u>

On October 8th 2013 one of the most
beautiful dream like beings, I have ever
had the honour to meet passed away in
Eastern Tibet. His life was the perfect
example of the dharma, free from self
cherishing with wisdom and compassion,
dedicating his life to the welfare of all
beings. Helping literally thousands with
the charity 'Rokpa'.

He was my first Tibetan teacher and he
opened my eyes to emptiness and the
actual nature of reality. Yet whilst
recognising the dream like nature of this
world he also did more than anyone I ever
met to embody compassion in everyday
life. I miss him amongst the primordial
bones of being.

I spent time in Tibet with him, he shared the wisdom of Tibetan medicine over many years in Scotland, his kindness knew no bounds. Everyday his vision inspires me!

Em Ah Ho!

To one of the kindest, humblest,
loving beings i have ever met,
a rare star in the deep blue sky.

May a wild ocean of immeasurable blessings, fall like rainbows from the sky like awareness, you whose words are like nectar, on the ocean of being.

May ten thousand raindrops,
of Buddhas blessings,
fall into your hearts
infinite compassion,
may all realise the bliss of being.

You who showed me
the clarity of wisdom,
and held my hand,
when i was lost,
under dark clouds of ignorance.

You who shone
as Padmasambhava's light,
a treasure to all beings,
giving your life,
to alleviate the suffering of beings.

No words can describe the loss,
when the sun falls from the sky,
and the moon has hidden her gaze,
and even the stars grieve for such beauty.

To realise
That which
opened the mind
to its radiant natural state.

Knowing
That there is no other
As everything
Is the shining mirror of awareness.

Marpa, king of medicine,
granter of ten thousand wishes,
you will always, always,
live in my vast open heart...

The Tibetan Coat

I am Akong Rinpoche

'Will you make me a coat
that looks respectable and rich

yet able to keep out
the winter of Eastern Tibet.'

We began to make a coat

gold brocade on the outside

three linings on the inside.

Rabbit fur, moss green wool

and a silken peacock blue

for the final trim.

We stitched and tacked and tailored

and stayed up nights

till we were sure

It would keep out the chill of the winds,
the cold of the snows

and still look respectable.

Finally we fitted him
with the coat before he left.

To top it, a matching hat.

Months later
when the snows had melted

he returned without the coat.

And when I asked him,
he said
'I never intended to wear it.

It was for the old man

high up on the plateau.'

By Angela McCabe

<u>"Your love of possession
is your disease."</u>

The great Hunkpapa Lakota Sioux holy
man Sitting Bull resisted forced
settlement on reservations in the 1870s.
In 1877, after he defeated General Custer
at Little Bighorn, he decided to migrate to
Canada. He had mixed feelings about such
migration as he pronounced the following
words:

"Behold my brothers, the Spring has
come; the earth has received the embraces
of the sun and we shall soon see the
results of that love.

Every seed is awakened and so has all
animal life. It is through this mysterious
power that we too have our being, and we
therefore yield to our neighbors, even our

animal neighbours, the same right as
ourselves, to inhabit this land.

Yet, hear me, people, we have now to deal
with another race – small and feeble when
our fathers first met them but now great
and overbearing. Strangely enough they
have a mind to till the soil and the love of
possession is a disease with them. These
people have made many rules that the rich
may break but the poor may not. T

hey take their tithes from the poor and
weak to support the rich and those who
rule.

They claim this mother of ours, the earth,
for their own and fence their neighbors
away; they deface her with their buildings
and their refuse. The nation is like a
spring freshet that overruns its banks and
destroys all that are in its path.

We cannot dwell side by side. Only seven years ago we made a treaty by which we were assured that the buffalo country should be left to us forever. Now they threaten to take that away from us. My brothers, shall we submit or shall we say to them:

"First kill me before you take possession of my Fatherland
Your love of possession is your disease."

Feathered Longing

The light of dusk, falls on the feathered
longing of a thousand crows. Who at the
turn of Autumn evenings, claw their beaks
to the tethered earth, in huge murderous
tribes of cackle and crags.

The shimmer of webs caught between
chestnut dusk light and the rustle of deer
in the deep ivy forest, purr inside the
heart.

The world an invitation to feel even
deeper the moist, broken rock and bone.

Sun sets, the cold curls her breathe along
the ancient downs, butterflies who were
just a moment away dancing with a horde
of tiny insects, set sail to no one knows
where.

Ecstasy sleeps in the tiny fragments of time before expectation and disappointment. In the timeless wonder of gratitude that opens even the most defended heart.

The flesh is the taste of emptiness on the sky. Born in earth and green wild fields.

Sworn by rain and the salt breathe of oceans.

This is all.

Twenty – Twenty

It's not hard now

To close the heart

And stir up

The mind

With all these

Arrows of division

Flying around

Words are cheap

They have lost their value

Bargain basement bastions

For one dollar leaders

So far from the mark

Of what we all yearn for

Yet pulled in by

Sermons of soothsayers

That know neither

The cure nor the remedy

To their own fakery

The wounded one

Easily gets swayed

By false icons

And golden promises of Eden

Yet deep in the forest

Of being

There are forests burning

Coral reefs dying

Tigers weeping

Whales sighing

Whilst we bicker

Over the scraps

Of someone else's dream,

Where flying to Mars

Is more important

Than diving

Deep amongst the contours

Of the heart

What kind of madness

Came upon us

Like great amnesiacs

Forgetting that beauty

Who gave birth to this radiance

From the explosion of stars

From the woven myriad of time

From the great potion of unknown

From the mystery of being

What madness came upon us

To get caught in a net

Of such tiny dreams

Spying on our neighbours

Curtain twitching

Like we somehow forget

The flight of ten thousand starlings

The sunlight streaming on ocean

The dusk spinning her silver webs

The call of the last snowy owl

When will we finally hear the song

That's been weaving inside our blood

Before we were born

Amongst the great silence

The haunting emptiness

The roaring darkness

That breaks open

Even the strongest door

Step out of the cage

Gather roses for your shrine

Take your prayer matt

To the river's edge

And cry

Cry again

For all the dying

Wild

That no one has time to grieve for

Gather those treasures

And make a basket

To collect all the moments

That stirred your being

To remember

The great holy one

That you are

Now bring those offerings

To the edge of time

And offer it

To the great mystery

As a gift

Promising

To remember

Wanting nothing in return

Just the knowing
Of this immense wonder
You already have
Standing
Here
On the edge of your life

The man who has no imagination
has no wings.

Service to others
is the rent
you pay
for your room
here on earth.

Muhammed Ali

If you have enjoyed these word spells, you can find out more at the following

links:

https://www.facebook.com/dejahu

https://www.instagram.com/dejahu/

www.in2wild.com

www.wildest-dreaming.com

www.wilderlands.co.uk

Printed in Great Britain
by Amazon

54411066R00166